Saltwate

JOHN MORIARTY was born around 1938 in Borroloola, in Australia's Northern Territory. In 1942, he was taken from his mother by government welfare agencies implementing the official policy of assimilation, and placed in children's homes on the outskirts of Sydney. After attending schools there and in Adelaide, he trained as an elite soccer player for state and national teams, but his sporting career was cut short by injury.

John became South Australia's first Aboriginal university graduate, gaining a Bachelor of Arts degree in 1970. He subsequently took up the political cause of indigenous people through the Aboriginal Affairs bureaucracy at state and national levels. A Churchill Fellow, and Doctor of the University of South Australia, John's board appointments include chair of the National Aboriginal Sports Corporation of Australia and vice-chairman of the Commercial Development Corporation. He was awarded the Advance Australia Award for Services to Industry and Commerce in 1995, and the Order of Australia in 2000.

In 1983 John established the Balarinji Design Studio, which celebrates Aboriginal heritage through contemporary Australian design. Balarinji has since achieved a prestigious national and international profile – most notably through the Wunala and Nalanji Dreaming Qantas 747 aircraft.

Over the years John has found his way back to his tribal roots, becoming a leader in the bush and the city. He currently lives in Sydney, with his wife, Ros, and their three children, Tim, James and Julia.

PRAISE FOR *SALTWATER FELLA*

'This is not a "black" book or a "white" book. It is a profoundly Australian book, as Frank McCourt's book *Angela's Ashes* is a quintessentially Irish book. It is about humans, and adversity and love, lots of love.'
Sunday Telegraph

'*Saltwater Fella* is sharply observant and keenly reflective. Moriarty's voice is warm, open, passionate and quickly engaging . . . this is an important Australian story, told by a natural storyteller.'
Australian Bookseller & Publisher

'Few Australians understand both sides of that gulf (between black and white Australia) the way John Moriarty does.'
Adelaide Advertiser

'Moriarty, despite the hurdles in his life, remains unequivocally optimistic. *Saltwater Fella* details his often painful search for his Irish father and his reunion with his mother . . . he speaks of these often intolerable circumstances with an astonishing lack of bitterness.'
Herald Sun

Saltwater Fella

John Moriarty
with
Evan McHugh

VIKING

Viking
Penguin Books Australia Ltd
487 Maroondah Highway, PO Box 257
Ringwood, Victoria 3134, Australia
Penguin Books Ltd
Harmondsworth, Middlesex, England
Penguin Putnam Inc.
375 Hudson Street, New York, New York 10014, USA
Penguin Books Canada Limited
10 Alcorn Avenue, Toronto, Ontario, Canada, M4V 3B2
Penguin Books (NZ) Ltd
Cnr Rosedale and Airborne Roads, Albany, Auckland, New Zealand
Penguin Books (South Africa) (Pty) Ltd
5 Watkins Street, Denver Ext 4, 2094, South Africa
Penguin Books India (P) Ltd
11, Community Centre, Panchsheel Park, New Delhi 110 017, India

First published by Penguin Books Australia Ltd 2000

5 7 9 10 8 6 4

Designed by John Canty, Penguin Design Studio
Calligraphy by Mariko Jesse
Typeset in 12/18 pt Adobe Garamond by Post Pre-press Group, Brisbane
Made and printed in Australia by Australian Print Group, Maryborough, Victoria

National Library of Australia
Cataloguing-in-Publication data:

Moriarty, John.
Saltwater fella.

Includes index.
ISBN 0 670 87865 0.

1. Moriarty, John. 2. Balarinji Design. 3. Aborigines, Australian – Art.
4. Textile designers – Australia – Biography. 5. Aborigines, Australian – Civil rights.
6. Aborigines, Australian – Biography. I. Title.

746.092

www.penguin.com.au

Australia | Council
for the Arts

This project has been assisted by the Commonwealth Government
through the Australia Council, its arts funding and advisory body.

Front cover: Wunala Dreaming plane (Qantas); John Moriarty as a boy, with his mother
Back cover: author photograph (Newspix)

To my children: Tim Bundian, James Djawarrawarral
and Julia Maraelu

Wunala

THE FIRST PLANE, THE WUNALA DREAMING PLANE, was cloaked in secrecy. It was wheeled out just before its first flight, when it flew to Kansai Airport, Japan. It landed at dusk on a very still evening. As it came in, you could barely see the plane in the distance but as it came closer you could see the colours emerging on it. It came closer and closer and you could see the brightness, the different colours and the bold designs of the plane coming through. It looked fantastic.

Hundreds of people were gathered at the airport terminal for the arrival and as the plane came up to the terminal, the cameras started flashing. As the plane taxied into its gate they all thundered towards it; people were running towards where the Wunala Dreaming plane was docking. Then the doors of the plane opened and the first three people to come off were my relations – black, dressed in their tribal gear, with ceremonial paint on, playing a didgeridoo and clap sticks, dancing for the arrival of this plane. For everyone there it was one astonishing sight after another.

Dreaming

The next day in the *Yomiuri Shimbun*, the major daily newspaper in Tokyo, with a circulation of 10 million, the front-page story was about Wunala Dreaming. The Japanese press gave saturation coverage to the arrival of this new plane. It had such impact that although it was designed to have the paint on for three months at the most, it's still on now, more than five years later.

Whenever I see that plane I half-sing, 'Wunala, Wunala,' the way my mother pronounced it. When I first saw the plane I sort of melted inwardly. It's a feeling you don't get very often – it makes you feel humble, elated, secure. It makes you feel all those things. It's happiness, I suppose.

Of course, having such an icon within an Australian company of such standing is a satisfying feeling. I don't think it's a feeling of triumph, really. I think of the hard times still, but I think of the Qantas plane as representing one of the good times. It's meant a great deal in my struggle to promote my culture.

Contents

Acknowledgements

With special thanks to Evan McHugh for his professionalism and support in turning my intentions into reality. He structured my book, guided my deliberations on content, and worked beside me to finish it. He responded to my emotions along the way with a sensitivity and friendship that I am deeply grateful for.

Thanks to my wife Ros for her selfless support during countless hours of recording and collating information, despite spending countless more hours attending to the family and our business. She encouraged me with patience and love through often delicate and painful memories.

I am grateful to Penguin – to publisher Clare Forster for her conviction that I should tell my story, and to editor Alison Cowan for her thoughtful, skilled support.

Thank you to my extended Aboriginal and Irish families, and my many friends and mentors in Australia and elsewhere, who have encouraged me and shaped my life through childhood, sport, politics and career. Their belief in me and their love have sustained me.

Prologue

Who I am

My mother with her mother and
father (my grandparents)

THE LIFE THAT I WAS BORN INTO, and should have grown up in, was totally tribal. In the early years it was all I knew. On my mother's side, my grandfather, a tracker with the name Publican Charlie, had been born near Norman- ton, in the Gulf of Carpentaria in Queensland. He belonged to the Kalkadoon tribe. He moved across from Normanton to Burketown and on to Borroloola in the Northern Territory. That's where my grandmother was. She was a Mara tribeswoman.

The Mara, Yanyuwa, Binbinga, Gudanji and Garawa tribes are all very close, as is the Alawa tribe from Roper River. We're a bit of a mixture in that sense. From the traditional side the relationships are very strong because of the Rainbow Snake Dreaming and the Kunapipi ceremony. My grandfather came across from Normanton to Borroloola on the Rainbow Snake Dreaming track. My mum, who was Mara–Kalkadoon but saw herself primarily as a Yanyuwa, was a product of that relationship.

I'm a Yanyuwa person. By saying that, I automatically relate to the coastal region around Borroloola. I also consider that inherent to being Yanyuwa is a sense of belonging to my mother's Mara–Kalkadoon heritage, which takes me through Mara country as well as Yanyuwa.

My mother married my stepfather, Willy O'Keefe, which gives me links with the Jingili and Gudanji tribes. That way I feel quite secure coming right down past Brunette Downs into the Jingili area, and the Gudanji is very strong because it neighbours the Yanyuwa tribal areas.

My dad was Irish, from County Kerry. He came from a town called Blennerville, just a few kilometres out of Tralee. His cousins were in the hotel business. They had hotels in the Northern Territory and my father came out, as far as I can ascertain, as a cook.

Being half-caste, as we were classified then, meant that I would eventually be taken away, because I was paler in colour than my mum. It was a policy of government when I was young to take away half-caste children and send them to missions or settlements. The policy was intended to breed out the Aboriginal culture and identity.

From my father I got the name John Moriarty. For years, it was the only name I was allowed to keep. On the Aboriginal side my names are much more complex. I should start with my skin name, which gives me a great deal of strength in relating to different people through the tribal system.

In this system your parents' skin group automatically determines what your skin group is. Skin governs your relationship within the tribe and stops inbreeding. It's a very structured classificatory system that determines your relationships with others, and who you should and should not marry. The person you marry should always come from the other side of the tribe. You should always marry straight, as governed by traditional Aboriginal law, although there is a secondary skin you can marry under extreme circumstances.

Because my mum's skin group is Nimarama, I can only be a Jugadai – and Jugadai can only marry a Nangalama, which my wife, Ros, belongs to, although I 'raided' her from a Tasmanian 'tribe'. Our children can only have a certain skin, too. The boys, Tim and James, are Balarinji and our daughter Julia's skin name is Nulyarima.

Through the skin group system I am automatically related to others within the traditional Aboriginal system. Your skin group gives you authority in certain things, but at the same time you have certain obligations. These can involve providing particular people with things, sharing with them. It can mean having responsibilities to certain land. It may mean being Jungai – that is, a caretaker of ceremonies and land for other people within the group. For me this means Kangaroo Dreaming, and also Crocodile, although the responsibilities work on many levels. Kangaroo is a very strong one.

This responsibility makes you feel secure in lots of ways, but it also enables you to contribute back to your people and to uphold the tribal system. Everyone is part of the mosaic that makes up the cultural landscape, which in turn spreads over the country.

Who I am

Going on from there, at the right time you are given your bush name (usually when you are still an infant), which is the link not only with the land but with the business end, the serious end of ceremonial and cultural life. My name is Kundareri and my land is west and north-west of Borroloola, extending to the coast and beyond. My mother's authority also comes back through the Gudanji land. I can exert some authority in that land too, but not as much as others.

Finally, there is the name you are given first, when you are born. When I was born the old people gave me the name Jumbana, which is a given name, like John or Jim. The name Jumbana links me with the land as well, but it has a different connotation. When you die that name is not used for a generation or two.

Borroloola is one of those land areas that have what I term crossroad tribes. We have links from Borroloola down to the Waramunga area, near Tennant Creek, and they extend towards Normanton, right over to Wattie Creek, the Victoria River Downs area and round the Gulf to the north-west, as well as right through to the Myalie tribal group at Pine Creek.

You get songs and ceremonies that criss-cross all that area and in the old days you could replenish the blood lines by being able to raid some of the other tribes for a wife. When it came to wives, there were never any outcasts. There was no such concept as a widow. If a man died, his brother inherited or could claim his wives.

Borroloola is also a crossroads where many languages are

spoken that relate to adjoining regions. And there are many songs from those areas that give it great ceremonial importance. With those songs you can go a long, long way – sometimes the length and breadth of the country, particularly with ones like the Dingo Dreaming and the Rainbow Snake Dreaming. The ceremonies and languages can take different forms going from one place to another.

Musso, my uncle, was responsible for the Dingo Dreaming. He could sing its songs and they went from Borroloola and beyond, right down to Victoria. When I asked him, he said, 'It goes through that harsh country. Sand. No water.' Musso always felt sorry for the people that lived in those dry regions. He said, 'Oh, they're a tough mob to be able to survive in that area.'

Most songs can tell you about the physical landscape, formations in that landscape, the types of vegetation and the seeds you can expect to find. It's like reading a map. In fact, I feel sure some of those Aboriginal people who accompanied or guided the early white explorers were following Aboriginal stories. They already knew the way to go and yet they were crossing 'foreign' country all the time, from one tribal area to another tribal area, way beyond their own regions.

This was the identity and culture that I was born into, and it was what the assimilation policy of the government set out to destroy. It was an insidious, arrogant policy that amounted to cultural genocide. It was the stuff Hitler was made of, the things he espoused that are seen as abhorrent today.

People say, 'Yes, but it was a product of the times.'

And I say in response, 'Would you like someone to come and take your child away from you today and tell you that they'll give them a better life because you can't give them a "proper" life?'

People say, 'Yes, but you probably learned a lot more.'

Who knows where I'd be if I'd been brought up in my own culture, according to my Aboriginal side? I think I would have fought for my identity in the context of my personality and my strengths. In spite of what was done to me, I feel I've shown a few people who said, 'You're no good and your people are no good.' I've learned a trade, I've played soccer at the highest level in my country, I've gone to university, I've fought for Aboriginal rights for years, I've started my own company and raised a family. And all along I've tried to regain the pieces of the life that I should have had, the one that was shattered when I was just a kid.

I still feel angry and I suppose that anger has carried me through, too, in lots of situations. It also keeps me asking the difficult questions. Why should people be treated like that? Why should the system single out me, and my mother and my group, to impose its views on us with no redress? That's always angered me and always been a motivating force. There are many pieces of my life still missing, a lot more for me still to pick up. By virtue of who I am and where I come from, I feel I have an obligation to find out what they are.

Chapter 1

Taken

Discovering favourite foods as a
'Saltwater Child' in Borroloola

I WAS BORN ON THE BANKS OF THE MCARTHUR RIVER, across from the small outback town of Borroloola on the Northern Territory side of the Gulf of Carpentaria. I believe I was born in 1938, although the exact date of my birth isn't known. My official birthday, the one given to many Aboriginal people, is 1 April. April Fools' Day, which is indicative of the attitude of the time.

My memories of Borroloola at that time only come in fragments. Moments like being with my mother, having a drink. I'm in her arms and she's giving me a drink of water from her mouth, making sure I have water. Whether I was sick or not, I'm not sure.

I can't remember the surroundings so much, but I recall people being warm and friendly. I certainly remember having a family. My grandmother was very affectionate, and then there were all the other 'mothers' I had too. I grew up in a very, very secure environment. Boys have a lot of freedom in traditional Aboriginal society and can do virtually whatever they like. After initiation, all those carefree times come to an abrupt halt when they become part of the adult community. But as boys they are extremely spoilt – they are more than cared for, they are revered.

Odd things come back to me in different situations. There's the smell of a horse – no saddle, bareback. People rode into Borroloola where we were and hobbled their horses to stop them straying too far. I can still smell this horse. I'm sitting behind its shoulders with one of my relations. It must have been my uncle, or could have been my stepfather, I'm not sure. I can still picture those horses being hobbled and trying to walk, getting feed around the gum trees and the high grass, dead grass. It's bits and pieces like that which come back.

There's lots of sand, the coarse sand from the river banks where we camped. And paperbark; we used to eat off paperbark. I remember gathering paperbark, as well as lily roots, creepers and vines, those sorts of things.

Food is one of my distinct memories, food cooking on the open fire. I loved the taste of fish and goanna and lizards that were cooked on the coals and had that charcoal taste, so I could chew the burnt parts. Even singed and blackened kangaroo ears, chewing into them and enjoying the crunchy texture. It's the mingling of the charcoal with the flesh that tastes so good, whether it's fish or lizard or kangaroo. I suppose it was a tough diet, but we'd supplement it with bush fruits and berries.

I was often near the police station. I used to be always around there or the welfare office in the white part of the settlement, where my mother used to work a lot. I think my grandfather, being a tracker for the police, may have used his influence with the whites to get her a job as a domestic. Nearby, I can recall a tree like a mango tree. It may not have been a mango tree because it wasn't so big, but it had green ants on it. I used to play next to that tree day in, day out. I used to call those ants my chooks. Why I called them my chooks I don't know. I must've seen some being tended somewhere. I'd look after those ants but I'd eat others, the ones we call salty bums. You just pick them up, hold them by the head, bite the abdomen off, chuck the rest away.

We had lots of watermelons. We grew watermelons and vegetables because supplies were quite difficult to come by in Borroloola. They only came by boat. In the wet season they often wouldn't arrive at all, because of storms. My favourite food was turtle. I can still taste it. That, and saltwater crocodile, but we didn't get crocodile very often. Turtles, the freshwater turtles, are just delicious. I had that taste for years and years.

Dances were always an important part of our life. I was only a kid, a little one, but I can vividly remember the legs stamping and the dancing. Me with my fists all tight, and fast-moving elbows and feet. I suppose that could have equipped me well for my soccer footwork. Dances were times when we had to show our prowess as men.

Mainly I remember the women dancing. There are a couple of the bigger boys, but they are just like fleeting snapshots. I often wonder why I've blanked out a lot of these things in my mind, and yet they have shaped me for life. Why should I have only snippets of that when there are so many things I remember in detail?

My early life was spent surrounded by women, with all those extra 'mothers' and the way they cart you around. Even when I was getting pretty big I still remember being breastfed – not only by my mother but by other women as well, almost up to the time I was taken away.

I can't see individual faces; I can't recall them now. My mum? Not a face. I don't recall her face before I was taken away. I have no memories of my father at all. Apparently, he was there for quite some time after I was born, but then he moved away. I've since learned that at one time he was in the British Navy serving on the Russian front and that he could speak Russian, as well as Irish and English. I've been told he picked up languages like mine, Yanyuwa, fairly easily and was able to communicate with quite a wide range of people.

Borroloola was very isolated and white men and black women had 'bush marriages', even though it was against the law then for whites and blacks to cohabit. My being part-European made no difference to the way I was treated by the Yanyuwa, which makes the discrimination against Aborigines for all these years so ironic. If you fit into the Aboriginal community well, you're afforded all the privileges of that community and you're not seen as anything different.

I was about four or five when I was taken. I'm not sure exactly how old, but it was 1942, so I guess I must have been about four.

The pressure was on my mother, and on the welfare, to get rid of me to a mission, under the pretext of giving me an education. Rather than risk losing me, my mother decided to go with me to the mission at Roper River, almost 300 kilometres away. She had to leave her own land, although the people at Roper are related to us tribally and we have very strong traditional family links there under the kinship system.

I was expected to go to school, which I did, at the Anglican mission school. In those days the Northern Territory was carved up into religious spheres of influence and my region was Anglican; other parts were Methodist, Presbyterian or Catholic.

After what seemed like only a few days at Roper, I can remember getting on a truck in a yard. It was an army truck with huge wheels. I was at a building with a fence around it, a wire fence with brown poles, and I remember it was north-facing. We got in the truck and it drove away, heading westward.

There were a number of other kids in the truck who were also being removed from their families, including Jim and Rose Foster, Wally McArthur, Tim Campbell and Wilfred Huddle-stone – six or eight in all. In the back of that truck, nestled among big crates, there were a couple of other smaller kids and a couple of women with cottony, floral-patterned dresses. I remember their dresses very clearly, because my eyes were at dress level.

I think I had one pair of shorts at that time. I'm not sure if I even owned a shirt. Most of the time that I can remember in

Borroloola I wore no clothes, but at the mission school I'm sure they would have stuck a pair of shorts and a shirt on me.

On the way out of Roper River, as the truck was going down a steep creek, one of the heavy crates shifted and landed on my toe. I can still picture my toe all crushed and the toenail bleeding and me crying and crying. My big toe was permanently disfigured, although I was lucky I didn't have my whole foot crushed. Even now, when I cut that right toenail, it always slopes up toward the top. It's changed over the years. It used to have a ridge down the centre and it would always break in two. When I played soccer I used to make sure this toenail was cut really flat. Not that it worried me – I scored a lot of goals with that foot.

The truck went all the way down to Alice Springs. It took several days. I don't remember any stops in between, nothing like that. There was a canopy over the back of the truck, so we could only see out of the back. I seemed to be always facing the right-hand side.

In Alice Springs we went to a place called the Bungalow, which was the original Alice Springs Telegraph Station. We met more kids from other parts of the Territory, and people from Groote Eylandt and Roper River.

The Bungalow was actually a little group of buildings with open land around them. And round rocks, very round rocks. I hadn't seen rocks like those before. The trees were different, too. And it felt really strange not being near salt water. The smells were all different.

The next thing I remember is the railyard. I was there with my cousins Jim Foster and Wally McArthur and a few others; we all went to see this big, long railway line. There would have been a couple of other lines, but I just remember seeing this one seemingly endless railway track. We were standing there, Wally with khaki shorts on – and in bare feet, we were all bare-footed. I can clearly remember my cousins from Borroloola saying, 'Yes, this thing comes along this track here.' And we all put our ears to the line, listening for the trains. They said, 'That's one way you can pick the train up, even if it's far out of sight.'

Then we heard that we were being transferred in the train. It felt like an adventure. I don't remember a great deal more. We were bundled onto the train, and brought down south to Adelaide, which was used as a staging camp. We stayed there for a little while and then we moved on to a place in Sydney. I don't remember getting there, though – not at all.

In Sydney, we stayed briefly at a place called Millewa, which I now know was in Ashfield. It was a tall building – two, maybe three, floors high with a fence of heavy stone and iron bars in the front.

We were a 'mission group', being pushed from one end of Australia to the other. Times like at the railway line, when we were with our own mob, we seemed freer. What I remember now are the times that were good, not when we were being shoved here and there. Whenever it was done like that, I don't remember it that well. I seem to have pushed it out of my mind.

When you're young, you try to be a man. But a lot of the times when I was trying to be a man I remember crying and crying, just sort of weeping. My mother and my grandmother and my grandfather and all the people I'd known were very special. The security that I had had was a real security. Yet the aspiration to become a man was strong, even when I was little. I picked up a bit of glass once and said, 'I know, I'll cut myself to make myself a man.' But I was stopped by one of the bigger boys, so I thought, 'I'll do it later.'

I tried to be a man but I remember crying and crying. I can't remember a specific place for that. Not leaving Borroloola. Not leaving Roper. For years I had the feeling that I'd get back there, and I just fought and fought as hard as I could to keep hold of that.

You don't admit to being upset, especially to your peer group. You try to shield the things that are being forced out of you. That's why I still harbour most of my thoughts.

I recall the other little kids, 'Boofa' (Wilfred Huddlestone) and 'Bam' (Tim Campbell), crying together. It was when it was just us, alone together. Boofa and I had a lot of differences in those early years but we never fought badly; at the first sign of trouble, a problem or something, we'd come together. The three of us had mumps and chickenpox at the same time, and were all confined to a room in a wooden outbuilding. I remember being sad for them – for Boofa when he was sick, the same with Bam and the other little ones. When they were sad, I felt for them. I was in a similar situation, yet I wouldn't feel the heartache as much for me as for them. Being little, we were at the end of the line all the time. Things happened, just to us little ones.

Boofa, Bam and I were always left together – us three. Sometimes we were forgotten. We had testing emotional times together, and yet we tried to be tough and to be like men, from the age of six or seven upwards. Perhaps that's why I keep pushing myself to do things for others, I'm not sure.

During all this time, I can't see any individual white faces – not in the army truck or at the settlement. White faces to me were authority figures, they were bosses. You lived with that, you had to get around that as best you could. At every turn we were told, 'You must forget your language, your culture and things like that. Stop acting like an uncivilised Aborigine.'

I'm not sure exactly what they called us then. They didn't call us blacks, that was considered a really derogatory term. Yet the whites reinforced their authority at every turn, especially when we were little and they had total control over us. They dictated how we dressed, how we stood to attention. We were made to remember who we were and what our status in life was to be forever.

Years later, when I found my mother, I asked, 'Why did you let me go?' I was still angry about not being brought up by my mother, a feeling that even now makes it hard for me to be apart from my own children. My mother told me, in a very soft voice,

'My son, you were going to school. I took you to school every day.' As far as she can remember, I was going to school for about two or three weeks. She said, 'I was taking you to school for a while and then I went to pick you up this day and you were gone.'

My stepfather Willy O'Keefe's memory of when I was taken:

'You see Johnny mob?'
They askin' me long time about you.
'No. They went to Tananbirini. To McArthur from Borroloola. They'll be back tomorrow.'
I tell old Pharaoh, my brother, Old Borroloola Pharaoh. Poor fella, countryman mine. 'Oh, they was lookin' for the boy.'
Old Mummy took you to Roper. The school teacher said, 'Take 'im to [school in] Roper.' I forget his name. It was a good name too, this old white fella. He come from Alice Springs, that old fella.
They took you on the boat, the Leisha. *Took you from that tree down that way. White tree.*
Night time you went. Gone now. Mummy went too. I went back along McArthur. Wait. Wait. Me and your uncle, Musso.
How far him? He comin' back? Your mother took you there to Roper River and from there [s]he let you go. And after that she follow you, [her] and that other old woman from Manangoora. Foster. But you gone now.
Mummy come back, she come back with the same boat. Bring

load, you know? She camp in Borroloola. I been in the station, McArthur. You, [s]he worry about you. [S]he cry.

Old uncle come, old Pharaoh. '[S]he lost 'im. You lost that kid, girl, eh?'

Old Elsie there, mother for your mother. 'What you gonna do? Gonna see boy?'

And I went drovin'. Me now. Musso and me went drovin' to Alice Spring[s]. Three trailer [cattle truck] – drovin' cattle. You were seen way out that way. Old Welfare fella. What that old fella name? We went to [the] Bungalow to see you there. You gone now. You went away on the train.

Chapter 2

Childhood in Mulgoa

In the cellar dormitory of
the mission home at Mulgoa

WE STAYED ONLY BRIEFLY AT MILLEWA before being moved on again to a place called Mulgoa, sixty kilometres west of Sydney, at the foot of the Blue Mountains. In the forties, when we were there, Mulgoa was a rural area and the mission home was an old, convict-built rectory, next door to St Thomas's Church.

The building was on two levels, plus there was a cellar underneath. The five youngest boys, including me, had to live in the cellar because there was no room anywhere else. The room right at the back of the cellar was dark at all times, so it wasn't a very happy experience. We ended up being in the cellar for about five years, off and on.

We were transplanted into a totally white community at Mulgoa. We were told at school that Blaxland, Wentworth and Lawson had first crossed the Blue Mountains in 1813, so the area had seen well over a hundred years of white settlement already. There were some huge properties around Mulgoa that had been granted to the early settlers, but you could easily pick the people who were badly off – they didn't have farms, and they had to fend for their families the best they could.

At Mulgoa we were in the care of the Anglican Church. Aborigines, with their deeply spiritual culture, come over to the Christian religion quite readily. Yet the missionaries at Mulgoa insisted that we must forsake our 'heathen' background. 'All those leanings that you had, you must forget all about them. You must not have your Aboriginal names, you must not have any of the languages.'

At first I couldn't speak English. When you're removed so far, as a child, and have to learn a new language in a totally different cultural setting, it makes it a lot harder. Even the older children and the few adults there were not allowed to speak their language. We kept a few names here and there, and the adults used to talk quietly so as not to raise the ire of the missionaries or the people that were looking after us.

A lot of the time we dreamed of going home, of finding our families. In a way I was lucky to have kept my father's name, Moriarty. A lot of the other kids weren't allowed to keep their names, although we knew who they were. My cousin Wally's father was called Langdon and he was a policeman back in Borroloola, but the authorities, who registered a lot of these births, gave him the name of McArthur, after the river at Borroloola. Millie Glenn, who even now is like an elder sister to me, was born in Glen Helen, near Alice Springs. Her name was given as Glen (she added the extra 'n' later on), although her father was a Raggatt, a white station owner.

This is the way the world was for Aborigines then. There was a lot of sexual exploitation. Aborigines saw a relationship with a white as being permanent, like a marriage; the whites often saw sexual encounters with Aborigines as short-term convenience. Not giving children their proper names was many Europeans' way of trying to deny who their children were. In those days, though, it was against the law to cohabit with Aborigines or to marry them. So everything was done in an underhanded way, and often the missionaries had to pick up the pieces.

We all pined, even though the elder ones kept reinforcing, 'Yes, you'll see your mother, you'll see your family.' Some coped better than others, but they were trying times for all of us. We were just children.

Although we were isolated from other Aborigines at Mulgoa, we did make very good friends with a lot of the locals, who quickly discovered that we were, in fact, human beings. We had likes and dislikes; we could laugh, smile, be happy or sad. We could be like everyone else in the community, except for being hungry and poor – though we were not alone in that. A lot of others around us experienced that as well.

I've blocked a lot of it out but I felt terribly alone during all those years, especially at night. During the day I'd be among relations and friends, the other boys and girls in the home, but we were there with no idea how long it was all going to last. I always thought that there must come a time when it would get better and things would get back to normal.

The reality used to hit hard at night. That was the loneliest time. I tried to compensate. I told myself, 'I have a warm bed.' When I had no food in my tummy, I told myself, 'Tomorrow will be better.'

In the home, the youngest boys were kept together most of the time – Bam, Boofa, Ken Hampton, Jerry Hill and Glen Roberts. Like Bam and Boofa, we all had nicknames. Jerry Hill was called all sorts of things, including 'Skullgill'. Jim Foster was the one who came up with the nicknames. He called Ken Walker, a white boy from Mulgoa, 'Chibarkee' and it stuck with him. I had a few names. Harry Russell, who had been taken away from his family near Alice Springs, used to call me 'Baggy' because I had baggy pants and bags under my eyes.

People were frightened to call my cousin Wally nicknames, though, because they'd get belted. If anyone picked on me at the home, Wally would stand up for me. We were both from the same place, close relations. Wally took that on, as most close family members would. Jim Foster would, too, but Jim wasn't such a good fighter as Wally. Jim was more like a Borroloola person – quiet, hard to raise a temper with.

I was lucky I was able to stick around with Jim, Wally and Harry Huddlestone (Boofa's brother, who was much older than us); they'd look after me. Harry was an adult when he came down with us, and was very dark-skinned, but it was considered that he could be Christianised and assimilated because his wife, Flo, was very pale. She and her twin brother Joe were both taken away: they were separated at birth, given different names and sent to different parts of the country – Flo to Mulgoa, and Joe to Charters Towers, in Queensland. Years later in Canberra, in the 1970s, I interviewed Joe for a job at the Department of Aboriginal Affairs. It was only then that I found out he was Flo's twin and heard the details of the long struggle he had had to find her again. At first, she didn't want to meet him because she considered him a stranger.

Although Harry was from Roper River, he was very close to my mother. They were closely related in the Aboriginal way; and he felt an obligation towards me, and I to him. I kept in contact with him throughout my life, until he died.

From what I can gather, we were on the books of the Anglican Church as welfare recipients and we also came under the administration of the Northern Territory, which was a Commonwealth responsibility. Even so, we quickly became a drain on the coffers of the Anglican Church. While it received a certain amount of money as a subsidy for each of us, the Church still had to pay for the person who looked after us, plus the domestic help.

In the early days all the eldest children were used as domestics and cooks, particularly the girls. The dormitories were kept separate – the boys were in one part and the girls were kept in another. When we got older we had to do our own cooking, and the girls had to do theirs.

Not long after we arrived I started at Mulgoa primary school, which was about a two-kilometre walk from the home. Mulgoa primary was a one-teacher school where David Jolly, a Scotsman, was the teacher. Mr Jolly was a very fine person. I liked him very much. He looked after me very well and I looked after him too, I think, because I used to do odd jobs like running messages and chopping his wood.

There was only one classroom to the school and six rows of desks, a school grade to each row, from grade one to grade six. I started in grade one or two. Having had to learn English, the grammar was a bit difficult for me. I still have problems with my English: every now and again I fall back into my old language; I forget words. But on the whole I did reasonably well at school.

As at all the schools in those days, we had to pledge allegiance to the flag. I was brought up on the Australian flag and the Union Jack and Banjo Paterson and Henry Lawson. That was the world I grew up in. Aborigines were not a part of that. At school, when they said, 'Yes, Captain Cook discovered Australia,' I'd often look around and say, 'Well what about us? We were always here.' I remember that at a very early age.

We were always hungry. I was often so hungry that I'd volunteer for cooking and washing-up duties, so I could sneak a few sausages or whatever was being cooked. Cleaning up, I ate the scraps. Even at school we used to be hungry. I hate to think about it now, but we used to look in the bins for left-over crusts of bread. A boy who lived across the road from the home soon became one of my best friends. His name was Brian Walker – he was Ken's younger brother – and he used to share his lunch with me. Brian used to get his sandwiches fresh from home at lunchtime and they were made from white bread freshly baked every day. I really envied Brian's lunches: he had the nicest fillings in those sandwiches – fresh cheese with pepper, things like that. I really enjoyed the pepper. Sometimes he'd have butter with peanut paste. I thought it was luxury.

In contrast I had a meagre little parcel of brown-bread sandwiches, often stale, spread with jam and other fillings. Some days we had no lunch at all. At times we were so hungry that we'd go to the back of the schoolyard at recess and lunchtime, down among the wattle gums, and eat the gum off the trees. We weren't allowed to go too far because the yard went right down to a dam but we used to sneak down there anyway. Sometimes we'd eat little grasses that we called plum pudding. There were grass seeds that we'd pick and sometimes we'd have a few little yams from the grasses as well.

One day the home ran out of food and they ended up getting food from somewhere during the morning. They brought it to the school, just to us mission kids, and we had to eat it separately. It was raining that day so we were eating under cover. It was embarrassing to be separated from the other kids, but the lunch that day was cooked – rice and stew, all served hot.

Things like Brian's lunches gave me some idea of what was normal in the community, compared to what we were getting. Things like that made you very conscious of how different you were. First of all there was the hunger, and then we were dressed differently – in old khaki trousers and shirts. We never had underclothes, or very rarely. I had one pair of socks that lasted me for years and they had huge holes in the heels. I used to fold the socks down to cover the holes in my shoes, but I wouldn't let those socks out of my sight because they were the only ones I had. Sometimes they got washed and sometimes, most times, they didn't.

At school we were always kept to our grade's lessons. In grade three, when Mr Jolly was teaching the grade-six class, I knew all of what was going on there. I could spell all the words and do their maths. I learned all their poetry and have appreciated it ever since. I had a very retentive memory and was able to recite the poetry that had to be learned by the kids above me off by heart. I particularly enjoyed Australian poems, the rhythm and the imagery they conjured in my mind. The bush was part of that – Banjo Paterson, Henry Lawson, Dorothea Mackellar. However, that's also when I realised you could learn more than you were actually being taught – and yet you were never given the opportunity to learn that much more.

One day, as we were walking to school, two of the girls from the home had a crust of bread, and they said, 'You want a bit?'

I said, 'Yeah.' It was a bit of dry bread, nothing else, but I was so hungry. I said, 'Yeah, I'll have some.' I was very shy then, a very shy individual. At the time I was keen on this girl at school called Shirley Ryan. She had long, fair plaits. I don't think she ever knew that I was keen on her, it was one of those sorts of relationships.

So the girls said, 'Tell us if you like Shirley Ryan.'

I wouldn't have told anyone normally, but I really wanted a bit of that bread.

And the girls said, 'If you say yes, you'll get some bread.'

I couldn't make myself say yes, so I wrote a 'Y' on the dirt road with my foot, to say yes. I did it for a bit of bread.

That's my first inkling of liking a girl. I thought she was one of the prettiest girls at school.

The home at Mulgoa was very staid. The area was quiet country – isolated and insular. The strongest characteristics of the place were hunger and religion, which are fairly potent issues to be exposed to at such a tender age. We were being brought up in a little enclave. The only places I ever visited outside the home were Brian Walker's house, just to go in and out, and the houses of some other boys from school – John Brunton, Rex Eisenhuth and Ken Baker. They were the only places I recall going to, and I never stayed long – probably just had a drink of water and that was about it. At the home we were pretty well made to feel outside of society, outside of other families, never part of anything.

At Mulgoa, we had three or four cows, mainly jersey cows, and we had the job of milking them. I wasn't that good at milking. Boofa was better at milking though, and I ended up looking after the chooks. I treated the chooks as my pets. I loved them. Some of those chooks would let me just walk up and pet them: I could lay them on the ground and pick them up and they didn't mind being stroked and cuddled. There were even a couple of chooks that would allow me to catch the eggs as they were being laid.

The chooks were fed bran, pollard and wheat. At times I

thought the chooks were better fed than us. We also used to mix the bran and pollard with some molasses for the calves that were born. I used to eat the bran. Given half a chance, I would eat the chook feed. I'd sit there with a big mouthful and say, 'I've fed the chooks,' but I didn't say, 'I've fed myself as well.'

In the home, Boofa copped a little more than me, mainly because he did things his own way and didn't succumb to their discipline. He wasn't as responsive as me. Tim Campbell was a bit slower than me in picking those things up, but he still trod carefully – and he was cute, so he got away with more.

One of the hardest moments for all of us in the home was when we heard that Jerry Hill's mother had died. We all felt terribly sorry for him because it meant he was an orphan. Looking at the situation we were in, we might have seemed just as badly off, but at least we still had mothers somewhere who we might be able to make contact with, later, which was good for us.

I don't think Jerry ever got over the shock of that loss. He became a loner. He seemed always isolated within his mind. I shared a room with him for years and years after. We got on well, we didn't have many fights, but I thought his circumstances were very much sadder than mine. I think losing his mother affected him more than we could understand at that time.

He was quite vague in lots of ways. We often thought, after his mother died, 'That's part of what you become when you are orphaned.'

I later learned that his family background was even more

complex than most of ours. His father was a white man called Ly Underdown who owned a hotel at Alice Springs. Jerry's mother was May Woodford Hill and she was a mixture of Aboriginal and Chinese. I'm not sure if his father had an Irish or English background. Jerry never pursued his father or tried to make a connection, even though we went back to Alice Springs on many occasions together.

I always felt as if I had a father and mother. Both. Because we were always taught that being born out of wedlock carried a stigma, the fact that my father wasn't married to my mother made me feel a bit ashamed – but it didn't diminish my desire to know who my father was.

Being Aboriginal, and my mother being a tribal woman, meant there was that obvious connection I could pursue, and the relations I grew up with always ensured I continued to remember my background and to relate to it.

While I was at Mulgoa I was asked if I wanted to be adopted by a white family. A lot of white families came in to visit us as part of the Church movement and they'd ask one or two of the children if they wanted to be adopted – because of their looks or because they got on with their other children or whatever. Jim Foster was asked by Archbishop Mole, who was then the archbishop of Sydney, if he wanted to be adopted. Jim said, 'No, I want to be with the others.' Then I was asked if I wanted to be adopted out. I didn't know who to, but I said no anyway. At least they asked us in those days. I was very thankful for not being adopted out without giving my permission.

Still, the system was at work around you all the time, controlling every area of your life. You'd want to get on with other things that you knew were out there somewhere, but you could never get hold of them, you could never find them.

It was in the twilight times, with dark coming in, when there was a time to contemplate life free of the stranglehold of the system. They were often trying to make you go to bed then, but it was at that time of the day that your mind was allowed to wander freely for a short period. Yet you always knew that you'd wake up the next day confronted with the same routine. Hunger, religion, discipline.

One night was different. One of the features of the rectory was a huge sandstone block, like a low font. The block was supported on a steel framework that allowed it to be moved around and the sandstone was hemispherical: underneath, it was perfectly round, and on top it was hollowed out to about thirty centimetres deep. The hollow held water, and we were told that the convicts used to be tortured by being tied underneath where the water seeped through the sandstone. Other times they were chained in the cellar where we little kids were sleeping. We were told that quite early on.

The front room in this cellar was where four of us boys slept – Ken Hampton, Jerry Hill, Tim Campbell and myself. Boofa, for some reason, had to sleep in the other room, the back room, which was dark even in the middle of the day.

We had grey blankets on our beds, which were like army bunk beds, the creaky wire ones with tubular-steel frames. One night I woke up: it was pitch black, the middle of the night, and I could hear these heavy, hob-nailed boots crunching on the sandstone floor in Boofa's room.

I thought, 'There's someone walking in there. There's a man walking in there, walking up and down in that room.' I had my head off the pillow and I was so frightened I felt I had my head up for hours, just listening. I was so worried about Boofa, having this man in the room with him, but I was too frightened to do a thing. I listened to these footsteps, pacing up and down in that room, for goodness knows how long.

Eventually, I must've fallen asleep. When I woke up, it was daylight. I raced in to see if Boofa was alright. He was still asleep. I said, 'Are you alright?' And he said, 'Yeah, why?'

To this day I don't know what that sound was, but I was so glad that morning when I woke up and Boofa was safe and sound.

Anglicanism was pretty much the state religion back when white settlement started. Much of the landed gentry was Anglican, and the support system we had was totally reliant on those sort of people. They'd give donations and come to see us and pat us on the head on occasions and say, 'Oh, they're lovely little natives.' That sort of thing.

The doctrines of Christianity, I think, are very close to the humanistic aspect of what Aborigines believe. We like to live in harmony with the next person. Because your brother is your brother, there are certain things you have to do, and vice versa.

We went to church a lot, which was pleasant, especially with the ladies harmonising during the hymns and all those sorts of things. Those beautiful harmonies stayed with me for many, many years. The singing helped to make us feel secure in Mulgoa.

The Aboriginal women who came down with us from Borroloola took on very strong mother/aunt roles, just as they would have in a normal Aboriginal community in the bush. We looked to them for sustenance and strength. Things like love and affection carried over, I'm sure, from the Aboriginal life we had been living up in the north.

At church we heard sermons that went, 'Repent and ye shall be washed as white as snow.' We didn't know what snow was but we'd look around at each other and say, 'There's not much hope for me because I'll never be white.'

Not that they didn't try to make us white on the inside.

If you chose a way of expressing yourself or saying something, or even moved a certain way, they would often challenge you. 'Why do that? It's a primitive way of doing things. That's not the way you should be doing it today.'

The way Aborigines move, walk and act is totally different to the way whites do. It could be the physical aspect – like being agile, having the agility you need to catch a rabbit or climb a tree or something like that. Then there are things like expressions. When we accentuate a joke or something funny, we often do it with movements.

At Mulgoa, we would often mimic the actions of white people. We thought they were funny – how they spoke and how awkward they were with their movements, the way they moved their arms and legs. They couldn't move properly; we'd never seen such clumsiness. Most couldn't run.

Others, mostly kids, were normal to us. Some kids even adopted a lot of our system and we adopted a lot of theirs as well. Kids like Brian Walker and his brother Ken used to come along with us all the time.

When the authorities caught us doing Aboriginal things, such as speaking our own languages, we were often chastised. What I felt was that they were chastising in a particular way, but I'd only pretend to go along with that. I always felt comfortable with my Aboriginality and the way I wanted to do things.

That's where I felt quite fortunate, in being able to resist having my spirit broken.

It wasn't hard not to cry over fights or anything. You never cried over a fight; you never cried over a physical punishment or any physical test or undertaking. It was only over those very strong emotional issues like family, in the quiet times after I was humiliated, or when I was lonely, that I became emotional.

With kids you could always fight back. The humiliation in my view came from the treatment meted out by your superiors, the people that were in charge of you. You were powerless. Usually I did enough to keep out of trouble when I had to. Yet I was always told I was naughty. I thought I was just active. The other boys thought I was cheeky, but I thought I was normal and full of life.

Some of the missionaries were nice, but others were very, very devout and uncompromising. The move to have us assimilated completely was always there, day in and day out. 'You've got to become civilised, you must stop those heathen ways.'

The older women used to say in whispers, 'Don't talk loudly.' Yet they'd talk all the time. Constantly. It's the Aboriginal way, telling endlessly reinforced stories – all about what had happened. They'd tell us about the people, where we belonged, where we came from. That's how I knew my name, my mother, who our relations were and the circumstances, as they knew it, that we were living under. Knowing that made me feel more secure.

It was those women, Marie Burke, Alice Roberts, Millie Glenn, Margaret Hall and Melva Hamilton, who kept on about who we were and never let us forget.

The only songs the women were allowed to sing in their own language were the hymns that had been translated. One that Harry and Flo Huddlestone used to sing was 'Jesus Loves Me' in the Groote Eylandt language. I can still remember it:

Jesu cummatary na prung gu
Jesu cummatary na prung gu
Na prung gu wanga nai i jai
Durra laka ranaka na prung gu . . .

They were allowed to sing that, but when they spoke of all these other things it was discouraged. I don't recall getting hidings just for speaking the language but I do recall being told to keep it quiet, particularly by the women.

If we got caught doing other things wrong, we were belted. Usually it was a leather strap across the backside. One April Fools' Day, I got up and was really looking forward to my birthday, but first thing I got belted. I can't even remember what I did wrong. My worst punishment was not getting food. I'd take the hiding so long as I could have the food. They couldn't kill your spirit, at least they couldn't kill mine, but they sure could deprive you of sustenance.

Sometimes we were told that we'd be punished by God. That often made me think, 'I wonder how He's going to punish me.'

I don't think I'm contrary, but one thing that made me stand up to the white system, even when I was young, was that it had somehow stopped me from being what I am. I always kept it in my mind to continue with my true life as soon as I could. So even though we couldn't dance and hold ceremonies like we used to, a lot of those older ladies kept singing songs at night time and talking.

Hunting was one thing we could do openly. When you're outdoors, you're outdoors. All around us were farming areas. We'd use a lot of those areas with little restriction on our movements. Hunting – the smells, the taste, the bushcraft – kept me going.

When we were young we always wanted to go with the older boys, but often we had to stay with the women. The women were not very much older than us, but they were old enough to know some of the traditional bush ways. We'd catch rabbits, turtles and lizards – blue-tongue and frill-necked lizards – and goannas. We even found European carp in the creek, so we'd spear some of those. There were eels in the dams, too – and when the water dried up in the summer, we'd go and dig them up.

We used to catch things with rocks and spears mainly. The older ones made spears and woomeras at first and then showed us. We had an idea anyway. Even though I was only about four or five when I left Borroloola, it was an important part of the Aboriginal way that I learned all those things.

At one point a missionary brought out a lot of spears and artefacts from New Guinea. The things that impressed us most were the huge barbs on the spears; they were made from the quills of porcupines. We didn't have those sorts of things at Borroloola. We had the wire spears for fish – the shovel-nosed spear and what they call a hook spear.

We used to have a lot of spear-throwing competitions, just among ourselves. The serious throwing took place when Harry Huddlestone was there with us. Harry was one of those grown-ups who was very good with a spear and who knew the old system.

In a way Harry protected us. He took us out hunting and made sure we were all okay. He was a born leader, though quietly spoken. I was told I used to talk a lot in those days, but I had that knocked out of me coming through the system. I shut up nowadays.

Harry embraced the Christian religion and yet he still taught us a lot about who we were. He had been a pearl diver up in the Gulf of Carpentaria. When we were hunting with him in the paddocks around Mulgoa, he'd take out a pocket knife and carve a boat out of a piece of willow tree. He'd make replicas of the pearling luggers he'd sailed on in the Gulf of Carpentaria and the Arafura Sea.

Like Harry, Jim Foster could throw a spear very well and had a lot of the skills of bushcraft. I can still picture him with one of the spears he made. We were out hunting rabbits and he threw that spear and it travelled very true and straight, with the correct movement in the air. We used to call it a wobble, the flexibility as it moved through the air that makes it go with such power and direction. Spot on. He was very good at that.

There was one time when this rabbit was running at full speed across the paddock and Jim skewered it right on one of the barbed New Guinea spears. He couldn't get the rabbit off unless he dragged it along the full length of the spear, because of the barbs. There he was walking back to camp, laughing his head off with this rabbit skewered on this huge New Guinea spear.

We caught rabbits with our hands as well in those days. Or with a rock. Catching rabbits by hand is easy. You know where they are. You can see them. You sneak up real close to them, then you make a grab. Things like that are very Aboriginal – moving without being seen to be moving, and the quietness that comes with it.

Another creature that can be caught by hand is a goanna, but it's a lot different to a rabbit. A goanna is one of those creatures that casts its mind around a lot more. You've got to concentrate on him at all times. You can move to a goanna while he's on the ground, or even on a tree, as though you're not moving. Just slowly, quietly. When he looks away, you can make that slow, slow movement towards him. That's the way you catch goannas by hand.

If they run up a tree, all you have to do is climb up after them. Or knock them down. If the tree's a big one, that's a bit hard, but I've known a couple of the women to chase goannas up trees as high as eighteen metres.

Alice Roberts, one of my relations from Roper River, did it once at Mulgoa. Alice climbed up this tree on an adjacent property and grabbed this goanna by the tail, right at the top of this big, dead tree. Hanging on with one hand, she pulled the goanna from the top, whacked it on the trunk a couple of times and dropped it to where we were waiting down below. We grabbed it, threw it on the fire and cooked it.

Those sorts of skills always stuck with us, but goannas are few and far between now. I don't eat bush foods anymore unless I'm in the bush and short of food. Then it's fair game, but I never kill for the sake of it. I think while I was at Mulgoa I was just honing up the skills I already had from Borroloola and Roper. I feel as if I've had them forever, and you just brush up on them as you go, as you live the life and practise.

Even now, when I get annoyed I still feel as if I should grab a spear with a woomera and have a fight with it. I've never had a fight with a spear, but that's how I feel. I know some of my relations have and some have died. I've never fought with a spear in anger – in practice I have, but not for real. Sitting around a boardroom table when someone's really having a go, I still think 'Gee, I wish I was out there with a spear with you, mate.' Where does it come from? It must have been there from a very young age.

I can still remember where all the good hunting spots were at Mulgoa, where you could gather food, right at the back of the schoolyard. We even caught a couple of hares down the back there, and a couple of rabbits, and of course witchetty grubs were easily found down there.

Even though we were supposed to be forgetting our Aboriginal past, one year we were asked to go to the Royal Easter Show in Sydney to throw spears and boomerangs and do some corroborees. We had to dress up in nagas – just a piece of cloth around our waists. At first I wanted to dress up, but when we got there I felt embarrassed because we were showing ourselves off to the whites, and I resented having to display myself as an oddity to other people.

Another time, when I was about ten years old, we had to go into town, to Sydney. I'd been down in the paddocks looking for rabbits, running around in bare feet and khaki shorts. I was down by the gate at the front of the church when someone yelled out, 'Come on! We're going to Sydney.'

Usually a trip to Sydney was a real adventure so I ran up and got dressed; my legs and my feet were all dirty but I pulled on my socks and shoes, and off we went. Someone said, 'Oh, you haven't washed your legs.' So I just wiped the top parts of my legs with spit off my hands to make them look clean from the top of my socks to where my shorts came down.

In Sydney we went into a shoe store, not to buy shoes but to buy a pair of sandals. At the time I was wearing my one pair of shoes, which were completely worn out – the heels were gone and there were holes under the soles. The socks were thick, grey, hand-knitted ones, but there was a huge hole that my heel poked right through. Usually, I just pulled the tops down over where the heels should have been, but I'd worn the socks out so much that half of them was hole.

Now I had to take my shoes off in the middle of a city shoe store and try to hide those socks. They were just terrible, actually terrible. I had washed them a few times myself and they were clean enough. Then came the ultimate embarrassment. I had to take my socks off and expose my dirty feet. After the sandals had been paid for, I had to wear them all the way into the Church Missionary Society office and then back to Mulgoa with dirty feet.

Another time we went to an athletics meeting in some suburb of Sydney, and it was a great event. Wally cleaned them all up. Harry did well with his high jump, Jim was good in other events. We did exceptionally well. I don't know the final tally, but the presentation was made at the Sydney Town Hall. Wally went up for his sashes and awards, Harry and Jim and the others went, too. At the end the only thing left was an award for Boofa and me: we'd come third in the three-legged race. Boofa and I were called up to the stage and there we were, two little kids in scruffy clothes and no underclothes, just these very baggy khaki shorts and short-sleeved shirts, and we went up the steps to the stage of the Sydney Town Hall to receive our reward.

It was announced 'Wilfred and John'. No surnames. Everyone else except Wilfred and John had surnames. Up we went. We shuffled on and shuffled off as quick as we could. Humiliated. The people clapped us as we sat down. I thought, 'Third prize is nothing. Being a third prizer, you'll never achieve anything.'

We were given a certificate and all it had on it was 'Wilfred and John'. Maybe I should have kept that and framed it. That's the way we were treated. There, part of it, but not really in on the deal. Acknowledged, but not quite acknowledged. That's the life we had to lead.

During the early years at Mulgoa I wasn't very friendly to most whites. I didn't make any friends except a few kids. Then, when I was about ten, Jim Potter was made superintendent at Mulgoa when he came back from serving in the Australian Infantry in the Middle East. His wife, Ruth Potter, was nice, as were Helen and John, their two kids.

Mr Potter was very warm and caring and he adopted the lot of us pretty well as if we were family, although he brought army-style discipline with him as well. We had to get up in the morning very early, at daybreak, and go for our run. We didn't have shoes most of the time so we had to run in bare feet, come back, have a cold shower, summer and winter alike. Sometimes we'd be running with frost crunching underfoot. We'd do running exercises and he'd drill us about personal hygiene. He'd say, 'You must wash with soap every day, even if there's only a little bit of water.'

Until then, most of the time I was hungry. My thoughts were focused on where to get my next feed. When Mr Potter came to be the head of the home at Mulgoa, he said the thing that had most impact on him was that we had no food. Before he came we used to have stews, rice pudding and sago, things like that. The diet was alright but there never seemed to be enough to go around.

After Mr Potter came I recall going into Sydney to the market in his old Chevrolet truck with 'Homebush Ice Works' painted on it. We bought heaps of cabbages, fruit and other vegetables from the Chinese traders. The next day, while I was hunting rabbits in the paddocks, I was carrying a cabbage and eating it. One whole cabbage to myself. I walked in the paddock and caught a rabbit, but still kept eating this cabbage. It lasted me a day and a half. I ended up having a strong liking for cabbages. I'm not sure whether it stemmed from this incident, but it did fill a very needy gap at the time.

After that, we grew cabbages and lots of other vegetables. Mr Potter organised the kitchen and we were rostered to do the chores. By then I was getting old enough to do the cooking, and waiting at table, as well as looking after the chooks.

I also used to help Mr Potter work on his old cars and trucks. The missionaries always said I was naughty, but if I liked someone I'd do anything for them. I did a lot for Mr Potter. If I was asked to do things by him, I'd do them.

Best of all, Mr Potter took us for holidays for the first time since we got there. The big boys went first. As so often happened, we little ones were left behind. The older boys always got more than we got. They had more food than us. They were given more jobs too, I suppose, but we still had to do a tremendous amount of work and had to look after ourselves as well – kitchen duties, gardening, feeding animals, cleaning duties, patching up, painting, sweeping, all those sorts of things, all the time.

Eventually we went on two trips to Port Hacking and I thought they were great – especially because they were to the sea, to salt water. They were the only two holidays I'd had. They were so good and memorable for me. The Port Hacking visit was to an Anglican home at Bundeena. We had to drive through the Royal National Park to get there and we could see deer jumping over the bushes, really high.

The home was right on the water on the south-western side of Port Hacking. When we were there we'd go down and fish, which I loved. We caught leatherjacket and a few bream and occasional flathead, especially if we were fishing out on the sandbank. We had spears as well and we'd spear fish out on the sandbars and in the creeks.

One time we were wading through the water and just spearing

fish in what's called East Arm. Jim was the best at spearing fish. He had a go at these fish and got a couple of big snapper. We were wading around and this fish must have been stunned by a spear. It bumped into Wally's leg and he jumped way up and yelled, 'Aaah, shark!' When we realised what it was, there we were diving in to try and catch it with our bare hands.

Those holidays were really special. And yet the fear of missing out was always there.

Chapter 3

A mountain interlude

The children I grew up with (I'm in the middle of the group, holding a puppy)

DURING OUR TIME AT MULGOA A NUMBER OF PRIESTS visited the home, including Reverend Harry Dormer. Mr Dormer was a priest at Mt Wilson, in the Blue Mountains. We ended up going to stay with him and his wife, Mrs Dorothy Dormer, at the rectory there.

The Dormers had no children at the time and they took the older boys, including my cousin Wally McArthur, Harry Russell, Jim Foster and Cyril Hampton, plus three of us younger ones – Ken Hampton, Tim Campbell and myself. There was about thirteen of us altogether. I don't know why Boofa and Jerry weren't chosen to go. I must have been about seven or eight when we went up to Mt Wilson. It's hard to remember the exact years I was there; we only stayed for twelve or eighteen months.

We were sent to Mt Wilson for two reasons: to break the group up into more of a family unit and to keep the girls separate from the boys. Girls like Millie Glenn and Rose Foster had matured. Joyce Herbert, Norma Nicker and Cecily Huddlestone were still young but they were maturing. Laurel and

Wendy Burke, Marie's daughters, were growing up, too. So they might have thought there was a risk of relationships starting, even though some of the kids were related to each other.

At Mt Wilson Mrs Dormer looked after us as if we were her own. She was a very caring person and looked after us very, very well, especially the three little ones. For a change, we were never wanting. Best of all, she cooked lovely meals. We always had delicious food on the table – roast dinners, blackberry pie and lots of cream. We used to pick blackberries around Mulgoa, but Mt Wilson was the first time I ever tasted homemade blackberry pie.

It also was a new experience for me to have butter – not just on rare occasions but on a regular basis. We were rationed, mind you, up there. We were also taught our table manners. At first the dining table was set with paper for a tablecloth; then, when we'd had a few meals without making a mess, we were allowed a proper one. The boys were pretty tough boys but soon we had a new tablecloth and we thought that was fantastic.

Mr Dormer used to enforce strict rules and regulations. He was very old-school, almost like an English public-school boy. He was very strong on religion and seemed quite academic. We used to call him 'Reverend Harry Cotterill Upton Dormer'. His real name was Harry Cotterill Dormer, from what I can make out; I don't know where we got the Upton from, we probably just added it to make it all sound rhythmic.

Mr Dormer was a very good athlete and the bigger boys reckoned he could run the hundred yards in ten seconds. He was very strong on fitness and sport. We got on very well with him up there in the Blue Mountains.

Mt Wilson was a close-knit little community and fairly isolated. I think it must have been quite costly to keep us there, although the fact that we were living in a home, almost a family unit in Mt Wilson, was especially good for us younger boys. I remember going to Mr and Mrs Valder's house surrounded by orchards. The Valders had two sons, John and Peter. John, who was the one I knew best, would go on to become a president of the Liberal Party and, later, a board member of SOCOG (Sydney Organising Committee for the Olympic Games). I used to play with his toys – he had these little dinky truck toys and it was heaven playing with them in his house. Mrs Valder used to feed us loganberries from the garden and give us scones as well.

Mt Wilson was part of the natural world, part of the rainforest, where there was all sorts of wildlife – lots of tiger snakes, all sorts of birds and lots of fireflies. That's where I saw my first firefly. At night there were pinpricks of light everywhere – it was a great sight.

It was also a good area for walking – and making spears. There was a little spot on the way to Mt Irvine where water trickled from one of the many mountain streams straight into a barrel so people could have a drink. Just nearby was a whole small wood of spears – almost dead straight. They took very little preparing.

We'd cut the right size off and go back and light a fire. We'd take the bark off, then on the fire we'd straighten them out, harden and temper them so they'd get a good whip, a good spring. We made woomeras as well.

One day when Harry Huddlestone was visiting us he had the idea of standing in the paddock opposite the rectory with half a dozen spears in his hands while we stood thirty or forty metres away throwing our spears at him as hard as we could. He'd just step to one side, flick the spear using one of the ones he was holding, and the spear would go almost the same distance again after he'd deflected it.

It was a test of manhood and we all had to have a turn. I was there with my spear, a very special spear I'd made. It had a real good whip. It was just my size and as I put my bodyweight behind it and threw it, it would go with a real wobble, a perfect wobble. I put all my might into trying to get Harry.

All the spears were rounded off at the front, which was just as well because if a sharp spear hit someone it would go straight through them. What we were trying to do was practise coordination and get our eye in. Also we were learning to be warriors who could handle those sorts of situations. We knew it was done back up north and this was keeping us in touch – making us better warriors, better men.

We all had a few throws and couldn't hit Harry. After I had one throw I ran behind him to pick up my spear and, as I was running back, someone threw a spear at Harry that went nowhere near him. But it hit me, hard, on the right-hand side of my forehead.

I can still picture myself being knocked backwards, my legs in the air and then being carried, crying, with blood streaming from my head. I still have the spear scar to show for it.

At Mt Wilson we'd spear crayfish, red freshwater crayfish, in the streams, as well as eels. Sometimes we'd spear some 'tubbies', as they were called. I don't know where the name came from but they must have been a native fish, like a native trout. We'd take whatever we caught home and cook it.

We walked all over those mountains. We even caught a lyrebird on one occasion. It was strange that we caught this lyrebird. We'd seen them in the bush but this one we caught by hand and kept alive.

We were told that if lyrebirds heard music, they'd dance. So we put a wind-up gramophone in the cottage down past the pine tree in the big paddock. All the boys stood there and watched the lyrebird while the gramophone played.

Of course, the lyrebird was frightened to death in this room, with music going and about half a dozen boys towering over it. Then someone had a bright idea and said, 'It'll be better if we put the music on, walk outside and watch it dance through the window.'

So as soon as the music started we all moved out. Half a dozen heads poked up at the window to have a look, but the bird did not dance. No wonder. We let the poor lyrebird go later that day.

From time to time we used to go to Lithgow with Mr Dormer. He took services there and on special occasions we travelled with him. He had a dark brown Dodge utility. While we were out in the white community, like going to church, I remember vividly how we had to ride in the back of the ute. One time we drove from Mt Wilson to Lithgow for a church service. While we were driving down the main street in the daylight, all in the back of the ute, we must have been a strange sight – a group of Aboriginal kids in the back of a ute with a priest driving.

At that time, I still used to talk a lot. I was talking there and the other boys were saying, 'Shut-up. You make us feel shame.' Eventually they stuck me behind the driver's seat, underneath where the cabin came down. The bigger kids held me under there until we got to the church. Even then, they wouldn't sit right next to me because I was talking too much and making them feel shame. I was bringing attention to them, which they considered wrong. 'You've got to be seen and not heard.' The bigger kids had that instilled into them. We little kids were being shaped that way, too.

I think I was in grade three up there at Mt Wilson primary school. Ken Hampton was in a class above, and Tim Campbell and I were in the same class. The school was very tiny; there must have been no more than a dozen children in total. And there were two teachers, one of whom was a lady teacher; I liked her very much. The school was in a very picturesque setting. It overlooked the mountains on one side and the main road on the other, which was lined with lots of trees. They were lovely trees, especially in the autumn.

I remember one cold rainy day we decided to get some wood to make spears from the area called the Barrel. When we got there we sheltered under a little hut to get out of the rain. Cyril Hampton, Ken's brother, was with us and he had one of those 'Billy Bunter' school caps on. He started clowning around with it. He bowed and swept his cap down with a flourish, saying 'rain'. Miraculously, a shower of rain came. After a while he repeated his performance, this time saying 'hail', and it started to hail. I thought it was incredible. Then he said 'rain' again and it rained. Whether he could see the rain coming, the first stages, or the hail, I wasn't taking much notice. But he was able to time his proclamations perfectly. The next thing he said was 'snow'. And it promptly started snowing.

We all panicked. We were a good two kilometres or so from the house, it was snowing and we had bare feet. We made a dash for it. On the way, I stubbed my toe on a rock and my toes were really cold so I cried all the way back but I didn't dare stop because they said, 'You'll get chilblains. Or frostbite.' I didn't know what chilblains were, or frostbite, but I ran like mad. We got home to the fire and warmed up. And it really snowed.

The next morning when I woke up there was snow in all the paddocks. I ran out just as happy as Larry. I can still feel that spring in my step as I jumped over the road and across into the paddock where the pine tree was, running along, enjoying my first experience of snow. Suddenly I looked up and almost ran head first into a snowman. I nearly jumped out of my skin with fright – it really scared me. Of course the bigger kids just laughed. They'd woken up earlier than me and had made the snowman themselves. That was my first encounter with a snowman. From then on we had lots of fun. We had snow fights and all the things kids do in snow. It was a magnificent part of my life at Mt Wilson.

Going to school every day we had a little routine. Mrs Dormer made cut lunches for us three younger boys and we took turns carrying the lunches along the way. I always did the last stretch. I'd have to wait for the lunch to catch up to me, then I'd skip ahead. The walk took us through a little avenue of trees. In the spring, during mating season, a magpie used to swoop on Tim Campbell. It would never touch me or Ken but it'd have a go at Tim. In the end we'd take Tim's schoolbag and walk on ahead. Then he'd run. He did it just for fun so this magpie could come and swoop down on him. Ordinary experiences like that were wonderful.

At school, the Christmas play was one of the few unhappy moments during my stay at Mt Wilson. The schoolroom had a little elevated area at one end, about a half a step high, where we had to perform the nativity play that year. I had to be one of the three wise men, kneeling at the manger with my back to the rest of the class.

So there I was, forced to kneel down and expose my totally worn-out shoes in all their glory. There were big holes in the soles and the heels were completely worn down. I'm not sure if they were the same shoes I had when I was in Mulgoa but they were my one and only pair. I struggled to kneel on that little platform while trying to keep the soles of my shoes flat on the ground so the kids behind couldn't see the holes, but it was an impossible task.

I'm not sure whether I was told to kneel properly or whether I was relieved of my duty as one of the wise men. All I remember is being horribly embarrassed. That's my only memory of that particular Christmas.

Mt Wilson gave me other experiences too. Hunting in those rainforests we learned a lot about the bush and were able to gather food. It wasn't like Mulgoa or up where we came from in the Northern Territory, but we learned about the environment very quickly. We learned where the snakes were, and we'd call dingoes occasionally. We'd call them from on a hill and they'd circle around. We'd track their movements and call them right in.

We also met up with some of the top axemen in the country. Tom Kirk lived at Mt Wilson and was a champion Australian axeman. I recall standing talking to him. He was a bit of a hero among all the boys because he taught us to fell trees accurately. He taught us to pick out the turpentine trees, the sassafras and the other trees.

There was a sawmill just down the road from us on the Mt Irvine Road. It used bullock teams: they'd go down to the valleys, along the peaks, and haul these huge felled timbers up to the sawmill. We'd follow them and witness that part of mountain life as well.

The community at Mt Wilson was very good to us. We were

seen as a mission, a little enclave within the community. I was sad
to leave, even coming back to Mulgoa, because Mt Wilson was a
land of plenty. We had more food and many more comforts, such
as clothes. Mr and Mrs Potter and others at Mulgoa did their best
to look after us, but it was different, I suppose, with Mrs Dormer.
She treated us so well, especially us smaller kids. She didn't have
any children of her own until after we left. Then I'm told she had
one boy called Marcus, whom I've never met.

I saw Mrs Dormer only once after we left Mt Wilson. She
came to Adelaide to visit us, just to see how we were. I was very
pleased to see her, and so were Tim Campbell and Ken Hampton.
We greeted her like a long-lost mother.

I'm not sure how long she stayed with us – maybe a day or
overnight. We showed her where we were staying, what we were
doing and how we were doing. I remember she cried when she
saw us and she cried when she left.

I'm not sure why they brought us back to Mulgoa from Mt Wilson. The oldest boys went back to the Northern Territory. They
were men really and, with their inadequate schooling, they
didn't have much chance to find a job in a small community like
Mt Wilson.

Harry Huddlestone was the only one who was able to get
a job, and that was at Warragamba Dam, because he had been a
pearl diver back home. Harry was such a talented man it was

a pity he didn't get a decent education. He had everything. He was a great dancer and a great warrior; he had a good mind and he was a lovely person with it.

After the diving contract at Warragamba Dam ran out, he was kept on with the Water Board as a labourer. He lived at Warragamba for many, many years. His children grew up there and his eldest son, Bobby, ended up playing for Sydney rugby league club St George.

Coming back from Mt Wilson to Mulgoa I had the same feeling of sadness and isolation as when I first arrived because I missed Mrs Dormer and the attention she gave us. She treated us just like her children, and we slept in a room with just three boys in it. We were coming back to sleep in a dormitory. In the cellar there were five of us, and there were at least five in each of the other rooms. I suppose the experience of being in a home made me quite independent. It toughened me up a lot, sometimes for the right reasons, sometimes for the wrong reasons. But when we came back I cried a lot.

Back at Mulgoa, James Stirling, Wally McArthur, Jim Foster, Cyril Hampton and Harry Russell were the first of our group to go to high school. Every now and again we'd urge them on, saying, 'Oh, they're going to high school. Fantastic. They're big boys now and they're going to Penrith High.'

Jim used to say, 'Penrith High, Penrith High.' He'd sort of sing it, and tell us all about where he was going to go. He was very excited about the prospect of going to high school.

They all did very well in their first year. With his sporting prowess, Wally was an immediate hit, and Jim was very strong on sport as well. Both were very good rugby players. So was Harry Russell, who played full-back. You'd never get past Harry. He had such agility and such judgement, and yet he was so casual, so effortlessly graceful. He would stop people in their tracks, he would tackle them right around the ankles.

Harry was always quick on his feet. At Mulgoa, after one of the church services, we mission kids filed out the main door of the church, then down the narrow road between a lot of tall gravestones to the rectory. This particular night, as we left, from behind one of these gravestones this person emerged, under this sheet, making some strange noises. We took off. We ran straight through that gate and headed for home. We were all frightened as billy-o.

We yelled, 'A ghost! There's a ghost!'

A couple of the girls screamed as they took off. They were shrieking, but we were running.

Meanwhile, Harry was killing himself laughing. It was him under the sheet. He sat on a grave and laughed till he realised that he was in that graveyard on his own and it was dark. Then he flung the sheet off, left it there and almost beat us home. He didn't go back to get the sheet until the next day.

That same graveyard was where we buried this little baby, Melva Hamilton's baby. It must have been only a small baby, only a few months old. The Hamiltons were my tribal relations, part of the group that came down with us.

Mr Potter, a couple of the other boys and I mixed up some

cement and made this tiny little grave bed. I was only about nine or ten myself. It was very weak cement, and I've often wondered whether we should go there and have another look to see if it lasted. I felt very sad for that family. I still do.

It wasn't long after we got back to Mulgoa from Mt Wilson that we were moved on again. In my mind it was a very short time, but it could have been twelve months or more. We were told we'd be moving back to the Northern Territory. All of us – the women, the men and the children.

It seems that towards the end of our stay in Mulgoa there were some very strong political pressures brought to bear on what the system was dictating to us. I've read quite a few press cuttings from around that time, from 1947 and '48.

People were saying that we Aborigines should not be treated as differently as we were. And the church was also struggling economically, trying to support us all.

For the girls it turned out that going back to the Northern Territory meant going and staying in a home in Alice Springs. Joyce Herbert hid. She was shielded by a family somewhere in the Sydney suburb of Pymble. They couldn't find her and there was a big hue and cry that this sixteen-year-old girl had just disappeared. The press made a lot of the heartless Welfare Department and the Church for sending back these Aborigines who had carved out a niche for themselves in the community at Mulgoa. Particularly newsworthy was the fact that Joyce Herbert was in hiding. Technically, Joyce was still a ward of the state, as we all were. At that time, Aboriginal people in many parts of Australia had to seek an exemption to be able to move in the community at large.

A few were allowed to stay on. James Stirling was allowed to continue right through school at Penrith and eventually became a qualified teacher. He was very fair in colour, and I think that was one of the reasons he was allowed to stay. Wally, Jim Foster and Harry Russell were forced to leave with us.

Joyce Herbert was fair, too, and I think they eventually relented and decided against pursuing her to send her back to the Territory. Others had gone out to work, like Millie, Nora, Rose, Ida Huddlestone and Nettie Pearce. They worked as domestics here and there. Also they took on nursing – I think it was at Ashfield Hospital or one of those hospitals near there. They used to come back to visit us.

At that time, no-one was encouraged to make contact with their people up north. Missionaries were powerful then and they were backed up by the Welfare and the police. We were all made to feel part of the assimilation program, and were not allowed to make contact with our people. I didn't know anyone who'd written back to Borroloola or Roper to make contact with their families.

Marie Burke, Alice Roberts and many of those people who'd been removed as adults eventually went back anyway. Harry Huddlestone went back to the Territory, but lived in Darwin. He made frequent contact with his people at Roper River until the time of his death. Margaret Hall, a close relative from Borroloola, continued to live at Lawson in the Blue Mountains, but I think she may have made a visit to the Territory very late in her life. I don't recall her ever going back to Borroloola, her birthplace.

When we boys were told we were being moved, I panicked because I knew I would lose my friends once again – my best friend, Brian Walker, and some of the other kids from my school. It hit me even harder when we were told we weren't being moved back to the Territory. A decision was made that the boys would be sent to a home in Semaphore, in Adelaide, that had just been started by Father Percy McDonald Smith. The place was called St Francis House.

We spent the Christmas holidays at Mulgoa and then, in late January 1949, we were put on a train at Penrith to go to Central Station in Sydney, where we were to catch the express service to Melbourne and then on to Adelaide.

Brian Walker and his brother Ken came with us to Central Station to see us off. I was very sad to leave Brian. I remember that the train had separate compartments with very beautiful leather upholstery. The windows were open and I sat in my seat with Brian and Ken alongside on the platform. I was making out not to cry but I couldn't help it. We finally said goodbye to Ken and Brian and I can still see them waving from the platform as the train pulled out. I haven't seen them to this day. I was ten then, almost eleven.

For years after that, whenever I was sad I used to console myself with the memory of hearing Marie Burke and all those women singing in the church at Mulgoa – they had beautiful voices. I can still hear their singing now: it reminds me of the love and affection that some of those women gave us kids. I missed that terribly when I left Mulgoa.

I think it was their affection that spurred me to get back to see my mother and my grandmother again. Often I thought my missing the women at Mulgoa so badly might have been a subconscious way of missing my grandmother and my mother. Those women provided the same sort of nurturing affection and gave me all the things that made me feel good.

Chapter 4

My first dressing gown

At Alice Springs, where I finally met my mother again,
more than ten years after I was taken from her

THE TRAIN WENT THROUGH ALBURY, where they had a meal on the platform ready for us, and a cup of tea. Then on we went. I don't remember Melbourne. We went straight through on the way to Adelaide, where we were taken to the suburb of Semaphore.

When we got to St Francis House, Father Smith had rooms set aside for us and gave us clothes, my first underclothes and a pair of boots. I thought I was made with all those things. I even got a dressing gown – a little maroon-coloured dressing gown.

They had a new terrazzo bathroom built for us, with a coke-fired water-heater that we had to look after. You had to stoke it up at night and the first one up in the morning had to open the vent, scrape the ashes out, keep the good coals and stoke it up again. This had to be done every morning and every night. That was our hot-water service, and it was a very good one. We were able to have showers. It was a proper bathroom with flush toilets and baths. It was very luxurious compared to what we'd had. At Mulgoa we'd always had cold washes. This was my first experience of regular hot water.

We were in what used to be called Glanville Hall, which had been part of Captain John Hart's estate in the nineteenth century. The hall was originally Hart's mansion but over the years the grounds had been cut back and walls knocked down. The building was pretty well intact, though, and it had a tower complete with turrets.

Compared to Mulgoa, Semaphore was an urban setting and that was very different for us. I missed Mulgoa very much. I cried and cried at night for friends like Brian Walker; I often used to cry myself to sleep, even though I was almost eleven years old by then.

The new kids in the home were different, too. They used coarse language which we weren't used to. There were a lot of clashes between us and them. In the early days at Adelaide I had a few run-ins with one of the kids, Charlie Perkins, and Wally stepped in on my behalf. I don't think Charlie liked him for that – Wally used to wade in and just clout him. On one occasion Charlie had blood coming from his nose after a fight. When he saw the blood he screamed a lot louder, then smeared it all over his face to make it look worse than it actually was. He was headstrong, and I found that a bit distressing. I had a bad temper too, but then most of us had – and I suppose I had a cheeky manner as well. I wouldn't lie down and take it from Charlie or anyone else. I wasn't big, but the spirit was there.

The others who were already at St Francis House when we arrived were there with the consent of their families – boys like

Peter Tilmouth, Malcolm Cooper, Charlie and Ernie Perkins, Laurie and Richard Bray, David Woodforde and Bill Espie. They all came from Alice Springs and were at St Francis House because their parents had asked Father Smith to take them down to Adelaide to school.

Father Smith told me that Charlie's mother, Hettie Perkins, used to work at the Bungalow in Alice Springs as one of the cooks. Father Smith met Hettie through his pastoral care of people at the Bungalow, and she asked him to take Charlie into the boarding school at St John's church home in Alice Springs so that he could have an education. Father Smith agreed, so long as Hettie paid for Charlie's board. Then, when Hettie brought Charlie to Father Smith, she also brought his brother Ernie and asked Father Smith to look after both of them. That's how they got to know Father Smith and were taken into his care.

At Semaphore there was Father and Mrs Smith, and Mrs Almond, Mrs Smith's ageing mother who always sat in a chair in the kitchen. Later, Father and Mrs Smith's son John was born. Mrs Smith's brother, Jim Almond, and his wife, whom we called Auntie Jingle, lived there too – I liked her very much and kept in contact with her until she died. Jim worked for General Motors Holden and liked a drink after work. He often came home a bit the worse for wear. One day Jim Almond baited Wally McArthur to try and hit him. Wally refused twice, then obliged on the third request with a short, straight right that laid Jim out.

It took me a long time to call Father Smith 'Father'. He

wasn't my father and I found it very hard to adjust to that. I found it offensive and it was not until many years later that I ended up calling him 'Father'. When I finally did, it was because I admired him. I felt close to him, and he was always good to me.

At the home every boy had a task to undertake – whether it was getting the wood ready, stoking the boiler for the hot-water service, washing up, clearing up, yard duty or tending vegetables. If we didn't get our jobs done we were chastised. Kids were fined part of their pocket money (which we never even got at Mulgoa). There were other consequences as well.

At mealtimes three bells were rung. The first meant 'get ready for the meal'. The second one was a warning that the third and final bell, which we called the rush-in bell, was to ring shortly and we were to be at the table standing behind our chairs ready to say grace. We all had our own places, and we had to sit in the same spot, day in and day out. If a kid wasn't there when the bell rang, he missed out. His dinner was on the table and you'd be saying 'For what we are about to receive', while others were saying, 'Bags the meat, bags the potatoes or bags the vegies or bags the sweets.' And as soon as we finished grace, that dinner was divided among the rest of us in a flash.

One day a kid who was supposed to have chopped the wood that day raced into his place at the table but there was no dinner on his plate. Instead, there was a mallee root. The message was that he hadn't finished his wood duty, so he had to go and chop some wood before he got a meal.

I used to enjoy getting up early to make the school lunches because that meant I could get an extra serving of cornflakes with rich, creamy milk fresh from our cows. Then I would have an extra piece of toast and make myself a decent sandwich for lunch. I'd cut it up the way I wanted it, instead of having two slabs of uncut bread. Often the sandwich would have barely anything in it because the kids who'd made it couldn't care less – except when they made their own, of course.

We used to be given margarine and it was quite rank. It had a horrible texture and tasted greasy. I could never eat it. To this day I won't eat margarine. And that was another reason I got up to make the lunches there – because the staff had butter and they might let me have some for my sandwich. They had all the luxuries while we had the basics. We often got the left-overs, which was why it was always good to keep in touch with the cook. That way you could be sure of a nice meal and you'd get first pickings of whatever was going – best of the meat, best of the vegies and so on.

When I started school at Ethelton Primary it took me a long time to settle after the upheaval of moving from Mulgoa to Semaphore. Ernie Perkins, Jerry Hill and I were in the same class, and there were a few others following us, so there were quite a few Aboriginal kids in that school.

There was a distinct difference between us and the other children, not only because we were Aboriginal but because we were very poor. Our clothing looked very poor as well. Charlie Perkins eventually gave me a pair of hand-me-down long trousers. They were my first pair. They already had holes in the backside but I promptly darned those, then I undid the hem and took them up a little. I ironed those trousers and wore them to school. I had to walk around with my hands behind my back, to hide the darned part, but I wore them anyway. I thought I was a big person then. I must have been eleven at the time, and I was in grade six.

I should have known those trousers would cause me embarrassment. At school I was always a bit shy but Boofa was a little bolder. He took on playing the big bass drum with the school band and someone else would have to hold it for him. One day I had to hold the bass drum for Boofa. He was beating the drum and I was trying to hold the drum behind me, so no-one could see the holes in my pants. Although I was embarrassed holding the drums, I thought it a bit clever, too – me being in the band. That didn't last for long, though – I was demoted even from holding the drums.

In grade six at Ethelton Primary I had an Irish teacher called Mr Little. I didn't like him and he didn't like me at all. I got lots of hidings, particularly when I imitated his Irish accent.

One time, when he said, 'Get your poitry booksss out,' I repeated, 'Poitry booksss.'

Then it was, 'John Moriarty, come out to the front.' There were about four rows of desks and I got belted up and down each row. He kept hitting me on the bottom with a stick. I nearly laughed but I managed to hold my giggles long enough to sit down so I didn't get whacked up and down another aisle.

At first, while I was struggling at school, Ernie Perkins used to skite, 'I'm getting better marks than you.' Ernie always fancied himself as a strong man. He often pretended he was Superman. He used to tie a towel around his neck, take his shirt off, roll his shorts up very high, then jump off the bed saying, 'I'm Superman.'

Ernie had a lot of pimples at this stage and we used to tease him. Ernie would admire himself in his Superman outfit in the bathroom mirror, flexing his biceps and shoulder muscles, admiring his torso. Someone would say, 'Look at Ernie and his muscles.'

And I'd say, 'Look at Ernie with his pimples.'

Ernie, in his quiet little voice, still admiring himself, would turn in the mirror slowly and deliberately, saying, 'Anyone who calls me Pimples out in the street, I'll flatten 'em.'

Of course, we cracked up with laughter, but that nickname stuck with Ernie for a long time until he got sick of it and picked a fight with someone. No-one called him Pimples after that.

In that same year we started to play Aussie Rules at school. I didn't like it that much. Maybe I was prejudiced because I was used to playing rugby league in Mulgoa, but rugby league wasn't played much in South Australia. In a way I was saying, 'Why should I cooperate with things here?' Boofa Huddlestone, who was in the same team as me, adapted to Aussie Rules much more quickly. He learned how to drop-kick with his right foot and then he began to drop-kick with his left foot as well.

Things changed in grade seven, the top year of primary school. You were seen as a senior then and had a little more responsibility. I also felt I'd overcome the disadvantages of moving and had adapted to the new curriculum. And I had a very good teacher, Mr Nelson, who lived at Marryatville. He was a lovely person and a top Australian cricket umpire. With Mr Nelson my marks picked up and I also started to have my own friends.

Even so, we used to get into lots of fights – especially when kids called us black and other names. One particular day a boy called Robin Johnson called out to me, 'Hey, pie face.' Robin was bigger than me, although he was in my class. I don't know why Robin called me pie face. It might have been one of the rare occasions when I was eating a pie and thinking I was pretty fortunate. Either way, we ended up having a fight. I wasn't very big but I stood my ground, wouldn't let up. I made up for not being big with a lot of spirit. I ended up hitting him on the nose and sending him flying backwards. His nose bled. I knocked him fair on his backside and that finished the fight. Both of us were called up to the headmaster, Mr Hansbury, and he gave us both a belting on the behind with the stick. Robin and I became good friends after that.

In grade seven Mr Nelson encouraged me to play sport, both Aussie Rules and cricket. For the football season, he asked me if I wanted to be captain of the school team. I said, 'Oh, no thank you, Mr Nelson. I think John Bartlett would be a better captain.'

Then he said, 'Would you be vice-captain?'

And I said, just for him, 'Oh, alright. I'll be vice-captain.'

Another time there was a school excursion to Mallala, where Mr Nelson had a relation. However, we'd found out it would cost four shillings (about forty cents) each for this excursion and we knew we were far too poor. So when Mr Nelson asked, 'Would you like to go?' I said, 'No, thank you, sir.'

Then Mr Nelson came and said, 'Look, your fare's been paid. Would you like to come?'

I don't know where the money came from but I said, 'Yes, I'd love to go.'

Then all the kids had to take lunches, but Jerry and I didn't have lunch with us so we had sandwiches at Mr Nelson's relation's place. That was my one and only visit to Mallala but I always recall the kindness of Mr Nelson.

In the home Father Smith followed a routine like Mr Potter's at Mulgoa – we got up early, went to bed early, observed manners at the table. We also had crockery and nice china. In fact when we first came from Mulgoa I complained to Mrs Smith at the dinner table: 'These cups are terrible, absolutely terrible. You can't even hold them properly. You can't put your thumb through the handle to hold them.'

What we had were fine bone china cups with those dainty handles which you had to hold between your forefinger and thumb and delicately lift to your mouth. I had never used such things before and she politely told me, 'This is how to hold the cup. This is the way to do it, my dear.' It was another embarrassing lesson. She was very nice about it, but ever since I've been very conscious of holding cups and table manners. Mrs Smith showed a lot of care and tenderness towards us and I was grateful for that.

Father Smith thought the world of Charlie Perkins – more so than any other kid in the home. Charlie was a boy soprano and he was encouraged to sing. Although we had singing lessons at the home, I didn't really appreciate them. I suppose if I had a reasonable sort of voice I might have had a different attitude. Despite that I enjoyed music, even in those days, when we had to put on an act for the other boys. They'd say, 'We're not taking up that sissy stuff.'

However, that didn't stop us becoming part of the choir at St Paul's Church in Port Adelaide, where Father Smith was the rector. The best part of the choir was that we used to get money for it. When we joined the choir at St Paul's we'd get two shillings for a wedding – and that was big money then. One evensong at St Paul's, Harry Russell, who was not a very good singer, was stuck at the back of the organ to pump it and keep the air going. There we were, in full flight, when the organ faded. The whole choir stopped. We waited while the choirmaster went behind the organ to investigate. He found Harry fast asleep on the organ pump. He was shaken awake and the organ started up again, so we continued with the hymn.

We left our mark on St Paul's in other ways, too. A couple of the kids carved their names on the pews and I am sure the names are still there today. A few of us used to exercise our teeth on the pews as well, including myself. While we were kneeling down we would sink our teeth into the pew in front and chew on it. I'm still quite embarrassed about that. I've refused to go back there to look, but maybe I should.

When Father Smith left St Francis in late 1949, they built a full chapel in the home. The wooden floors were surfaced but they put a heavy rubber strip down the middle of the passage leading to it. Other, more elegant homes had runner mats, but not us. We had this hard-wearing, heavy, rubber mat.

After Father Smith we got Father Taylor, although I stayed in contact with Father Smith for years after. Father Taylor had a length of industrial rubber hose, which he called Joey, that he used to belt us with – usually when we were showering, or first thing in the morning to get us out of bed. Needless to say, we were extremely happy when he moved on.

Father Sherwin, who followed Father Taylor, was just back from serving in the Army during World War II. He had a bald head, a prominent chin and was a strong old man. He was very much a disciplinarian, still living the life of the army – so much so that he went to the Army Disposals store and bought us all ex-army shorts, khaki shirts and army socks. We looked like little soldiers.

With Father Sherwin the bell rang at a quarter to six in the morning and we had to get up straight away. If you were on duty you'd already be up by that stage, preparing breakfast and the school lunches.

We used to have to attend chapel twice a day, in the morning before school and in the evening – and it was the scene of some memorable incidents. On one occasion Father Sherwin was robed for the Sunday service and Gordon Briscoe, another of the boys from the home, was the server. Gordon was standing in front of Father Sherwin, holding the incense burner. Father Sherwin shouted 'In the name of the Father', and Gordon swung the incense lamp towards him.

The second time he swung the incense burner after 'And of the Son'.

And the third time, Gordon got a little exuberant and, just as Father Sherwin was bowing, saying, 'And of the Holy Ghost', Gordon Briscoe swung the urn and it connected with Father Sherwin's bald head and cut him above the eye. He fell backwards – and Gordon Briscoe just about dropped the urn.

'Sorry Father, sorry Father!' he wailed. And there was Father Sherwin mopping up the cut on his forehead while the service continued. Of course, we all giggled and thought, 'Serves him right.'

Another time we were at the early-morning communion service at St Nicholas's church in Ethelton. We were never allowed to have breakfast before morning service because the bread of communion should be taken before any food. That morning, when we were singing, Vince Copley fainted right in the middle of 'Onward Christian Soldiers'. I was next to him and he just slumped straight over the pew in front. He looked as if he was convulsing, which prompted me to stand up straighter and sing with a lot more fervour. I thought he was being punished by God, so I continued with the hymn while he lay there convulsing. Thankfully, a couple of people raced over, pushed me aside and picked him up and revived him.

On school days, after morning service and breakfast, Father Sherwin always had us line up for inspection before we went to school. Anyone who hadn't done their job by the time of the inspection had to go and do it while the rest of us waited in line, standing at attention in the passage between the office and the dining room. Laurie Bray eventually got fed up with Sherwin and one morning he lined up with his tie on but no shirt. Father Sherwin paraded up and down, saw Laurie and blew his top. Laurie got a hiding for that, and we were all late for school as well.

Some kids were always late for school. I used to run the three kilometres to school to be on time. The fear of being late for school in those days must have done me a lot of good. I was dead scared of getting yard duty or detention after school as punishment for being late. Running to school did a lot for my fitness. I did it day in, day out. Rain or hail, I was running. I'd run past the stables where they had the huge draught horses which worked on the wharves. I'd run down beside the Vonotoffs' place, down Mead Street, over the Glanville Railway Station and on to the school. I'd do this almost every day.

I was too poor to have a bike. A couple of kids had bikes. Ernie Perkins had a bike. He and Charlie seemed to have a lot more money than we did because their mother used to send money down to them. I had nothing. Having been taken away from our parents, the kids from Mulgoa had no money at all. Since I was one of the boys who was totally dependent on welfare I had very few possessions, but what possessions I did have I really looked after. If I got a shirt or singlet or something I'd hold onto it until it was totally worn out and someone would have to wrench it from me to get rid of it. In fact I've still got the dressing gown I was given at the home. It was miles too big for me when I first got it but I've kept it. I still have it almost fifty years later.

I also had a suitcase, which I guarded with my life. At Christmas the boys from Alice Springs went back for their holidays and the ones left were the ones from the far north who'd been taken away from their parents. One year, Charlie Perkins asked whether he could borrow my suitcase to go up to Alice Springs, and I said yes.

The boys going back to Alice Springs would be excited for weeks before they embarked on their trip. They'd talk incessantly about how they'd catch the train from Adelaide to Alice, the 'Ghan', and what they would do up there. The 'Ghan' used to leave from the Adelaide Railway Station on Thursday mornings at eight o'clock. It was scheduled to arrive in Alice Springs just after lunch on Saturday. That depended on the floods and other elements on the way up. If there was a new driver on, the train might have to take one or two extra runs to get up certain hills. The train used to dawdle over different parts of the country and then she'd rattle downhill at great speed. It was a very exciting old train trip.

The year Charlie borrowed my suitcase he came back from holidays and it was wrecked. He often did that with my stuff – and I sometimes did not get my stuff back. I think he got a hiding for that.

At Christmas it was sad for us to see everyone else go. We

used to have roughly seven weeks' holiday. We were the forgotten ones even then, and we were left to our own devices. We would go either to the beach or to the sandhills towards Grange, where West Lakes is now. Occasionally, we were given money to go to Belair National Park on the train. That was a great day out for us. We'd go home with spears that we'd cut in the National Park and then we'd spear fish down on Semaphore beach.

I started high school in 1951, attending Le Fevre Boys' Technical High School. At the time the population of Australia was only about five, maybe six, million, and in those days there were very few immigrants of non-English-speaking background. There were some immigrants coming through from Europe, Italians were starting to come in larger numbers and a lot of what they called Balts, from the Baltic States. It was a derogatory term to call them Balts. We were told, 'Oh, don't mix with those people, they don't speak English. They are undesirables.'

We didn't come across many Aborigines in those times. There were a few down at Port Adelaide, where Vince Copley's mother and his relations used to live. We met with them on occasions but we were told, whenever we came across Aborigines, 'Don't mix with them. They are different to you. You have to be careful not to mix with them.'

As for us, at high school we were called a few derogatory names but after a few fights everything levelled out. Some of the older boys who were already attending Le Fevre Tech, like Wally McArthur, Jim Foster and Harry Russell, were pretty good fighters, as well as good sportsmen. They were looked up to. So after a few of their fights us smaller kids – we always used to be called the little kids – followed behind on a reasonably smooth path. They 'broke the ice' for us.

St Francis House gave a prize to the best St Francis boy at Le Fevre Tech. Before I got there, Charlie had got all the prizes for the best marks. Then, for three years straight, I won those. One year the prize was a bag, like a leather Gladstone bag. I thought that was a real prize, something I had earned and I really cherished that. I held onto it for years.

I still got into trouble a lot at secondary school. In my first year I was put into 1EF, one of the lower classes. I wondered why I was put there. I wasn't sure whether it was because I was Aboriginal or just academically inept. 1EF was Mr Lean's class; he was a Maori teacher.

Mr Lean was my teacher in second year, too, and he used to give me lots of hidings for talking or laughing in class. John Tregoning, who I sat next to during that year, became my friend. He lived at Alberton and he'd race off straight after school because he had a paper round. So every time we were told to report to Mr Lean after school for punishment, I was the only one who would turn up. Mr Lean would never chase John Tregoning to chastise him but I would always cop it. That upset me because it was so inconsistent. Another teacher I remember with mixed feelings was Mr Pembshaw, an Indian with a strong accent. Every time we did anything wrong, he'd pull us by the hair just above the ear – the most painful spot on the head that you can find. He'd do that just to punish us, even when our marks were quite reasonable and our behaviour was, I thought, very good. He was quite cruel.

My other friend during second and third year at Le Fevre Tech was Alan Thompson. Alan was a gentle person, very strong. Alan's father used to have a dragnet, a fishing net, and I would often encourage Alan to take the net down to Semaphore beach. We'd catch tommy ruffs and garfish, huge garfish, and we'd get mullet and even some whiting. For me, fishing was some of the best fun.

Le Fevre Tech was very much a working-class school, very much focused on equipping boys for apprenticeships – metalwork, woodwork and sheet metal work. Like some of the Aboriginal boys that went before me, I was destined to go into a trade. At the time I didn't even know what a fitting and turning apprenticeship was, but that didn't stop me saying, 'Yes, I want to be that.' Wally McArthur had taken that trade, and I looked up to him. Wally looked after me and I emulated him in lots of ways, or tried to.

Why we had to go to Le Fevre Boys' Tech was never explained to us. It was the school where people went who were going to do a trade. At that time there was no such thing in our vocabulary as university, higher education or a profession. The reasons they sent us to technical high school were probably twofold. First, it was cheaper. Secondly, we were not expected to do any more than service industry as workers or, at best, as tradesmen.

My father arrived in Australia in 1928. He is second from the right in this photo, which was taken on the veranda of the Borroloola Hotel around 1940.

After I was taken away from my mother I spent my childhood in a series of mission homes, with other children of the stolen generations. Pictured here, in 1948, are (from left to right) Glen Roberts, myself, Jerry Hill, Wilfred Huddlestone, Tim Campbell and Ken Hampton.

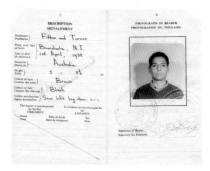

My passport. Although the exact date of my birth isn't known, my official birthday is the one given to many Aboriginal people, 1 April – April Fools' Day, which is indicative of the attitude of the time.

Nungas Aussie Rules football club. Sport proved to be a very effective way of uniting Aboriginal people, and I enjoyed playing with this club.

Receiving my apprenticeship papers in 1959 after training as a fitter and turner at Osborne Power Station.

My father's side of the family is from Ireland, and I made a pilgrimage there in 1980. At their house in Tralee, I first met my cousin (also called John Moriarty) and his family – wife Morna and daughter Maeve.

Bob and Hazel Hawke, with myself and Charlie Perkins during a NAIDOC week function at the Lodge, Canberra, in the 1980s.

Merle Griffin was a lifelong friend. Our paths crossed from my earliest years, and she was present at some of the most significant times in my life, including my marriage to Ros in 1982 when this photo was taken.

Old Tim, a man of great authority among the Yanyuwa, holding our first son, Tim. When he was seventeen months old, we took Tim to Borroloola to be given his Aboriginal name, Bundian, 'Cheeky Brown Snake'.

With James and Tim on the banks of the Wearyan River, near Borroloola. We often spend time there as a family, hunting and camping with our people, sleeping out wherever we go.

With my tribal uncles, Musso Harvey and Leo Finlay, at Borroloola. Between them, they taught me the ceremonies and tribal traditions I needed to assume my place in the tribe.

In 1983, Ros and I established Balarinji design studio, with the aim of celebrating Aboriginal heritage through contemporary Australian design.

Balarinji fashion shoot, Central Australia.

'Gecko at Sunrise', from Balarinji's Creation Journeys Collection.

The Qantas Dreaming planes, designed by Balarinji: the first was Wunala Dreaming, which relates to my Kangaroo Dreaming; its reception was so favourable that Qantas launched the blue Nalanji Dreaming plane the following year.

'Body Paint', 1996.

Painting the Darling Park Dreamcourt mural of pre-colonial indigenous trade for Lend Lease in 1999.

James, Ros, me, Julia and Tim at home in Sydney.

From the time we moved to Semaphore, the day-to-day re-inforcing by the Mulgoa women about who we were and where we were from was gone. The political atmosphere outside the home at Semaphore was different, too. We were not as isolated as we had been at Mulgoa. And yet we were in a home and that made us feel different from the rest of the community.

However, the policy towards Aborigines was gradually changing. Until then we had been made to feel ashamed of our full-blood mothers. We were told: 'They are not the same as you'; we were told, 'They are inferior people.' I didn't like that because it reflected on me all the time. First the missions re-inforced our supposed inferiority, according to their doctrine, then it manifested itself because we were not full citizens of Australia. We were still at the end of the queue, still called blacks, niggers, boongs or whatever terms people got their tongues around. We were still second-class citizens. We could still be transported across the country against our will, belted up or locked up and have no redress to any system of justice.

At Semaphore we were still technically under the control of the Australian Board of Missions and the Northern Territory Welfare Department. As we came from the Territory we were not subject to the same law as the other Aborigines in South Australia. We were often told that we should try not to be like the Aborigines around us. At the home, they'd say, 'Get your hair cut! You look like an Aborigine from Point Pearce or from Point McLeay.'

We'd meet Aborigines down at Port Adelaide and some of

them were drunks. You'd see them staggering. I saw the drunks walking around – white and black – but the black ones were more visible because they were excluded from the pubs and so they drank in the streets and parks. Seeing that convinced me to not drink because those people were treated in a very bad way. They had been ground down and I didn't like that. Back then, though, the people that drank in the pub weren't much better off, for this was the era of the 'big swill', six o'clock closing. Even when I was quite young I'd already decided that the culture and the mentality of the people at the pub were not for me.

At that stage most of the Aboriginal influence in my life was gone, except for what I was harbouring deep inside. By then, though, I was old enough to decide what was right for me and to begin to forge my links back to the Territory. The desire to link up with my mother and my family was always strong, but it became much stronger. That was when I started to make contact with people who said, 'Yes, you can do this in order to make contact with your mother.'

Although the superintendents at St Francis House knew we came from the Top End, they never encouraged us to write to our relatives there. Then, while someone called Maurice Wilson (whom we nicknamed 'Wicky' Wilson) was in charge of the home, Malcolm Bald came along, at first as assistant superintendent.

When we met Malcolm Bald through the Scouts, he was a young fellow, about twenty-five or twenty-six, and he related to us very well. He had been brought up as a Methodist, although he ended up working at our Anglican-run boys' home. Malcolm not only encouraged me to write a letter to my mother, he also helped find out where I could send it.

I can't remember all the words of that first letter, not the exact words, but it was apprehensive – something like, 'My name is so and so and I'm told you are my mother and I just wanted to contact you and meet you again.'

I didn't want to reveal my feelings because I knew that the person who would be reading my letter wasn't my mother. I had to write to her through other people because my mother couldn't read or write. That restricted me, too. I really wanted to keep things private, because we never had privacy anywhere. My letter didn't say anything too embarrassing because I just wanted to make the first contact.

I remember, though, that it started with 'Dear Mum'. I didn't want to say 'mum', because I'd never called anyone that – I found it very awkward to write the word that first time.

I was thirteen when I sent that first letter to my mother. Actually, I tried to write to her from Mulgoa once; it's a vague memory, but I did try. What stopped me was that I didn't know where she was. I had the paper, and I think I might've started writing, but it wasn't until I was reasonably confident of finding her that I could finally put pen to paper and actually send a letter.

And at that time I'd lost a lot of my Yanyuwa language. Nothing was ever written in Aboriginal language in those days (we have a dictionary nowadays), so I wrote to my mother in English and it was very guarded. For all the years at Mulgoa and at St Francis House, I didn't tell anyone my thoughts. I'd share a lot of things, but not my innermost thoughts. It wasn't until very late in life that I started sharing. Some things are still secret.

After I sent that first letter I was hopeful of getting a reply. Hopeful. But because of my inability to make contact for so many years, I was also feeling very apprehensive. I was still keen to make contact but I had doubts, too: Why did my mother let me go? Did she want me? Would she be able to write back?

Would she be able to make appropriate contact with me? Was it illegal for us to be in contact? All these things crowded my mind. My mother was still a ward of the state; I was still a ward of the state. She was a full-blood living in a traditional Aboriginal community and I was a half-caste (according to the whites' terminology) living in the city; there were different laws governing us. She was my mother, but the way the legal system worked at that time I didn't know if making contact could get her into trouble.

The Aboriginal women at Mulgoa and the older fellows like Harry Huddlestone were always saying that your family is important, your mother is important. In our system, your skin name comes through your mother. That's why you're always told to keep in touch with your mother.

Eventually I started to get letters from people saying what a good girl my mother was. Other people were writing her letters for her – people from the station where she worked, welfare officers and government people. They wrote to tell me that my mother was okay the last time they'd heard.

Even though the letters were quite impersonal I was still

grateful to have them. After that first contact, I started talking more freely about my daily life – what I was doing, where I was living – reassuring my mother that I was okay. I wrote about two or three times a year, which was good for writing to somewhere like Borroloola because at the time communications with such remote places were not that great. There were mail trucks that went through pretty regularly but in the wet season there could be breaks of weeks at a time. The important thing, though, was that I was happy with my knowledge of my mother.

While I was still going to Le Fevre Tech I started to go on holidays to Alice Springs and that was really good for me. We were able to stay at St John's Hostel while the others, such as Charlie and Ernie Perkins, Malcolm Cooper and Bill Espie, stayed with their parents.

I got to like Charlie's mother, Hettie Perkins, very much – and I became close to Charlie as well, even though we used to have many differences.

Hettie looked after me a great deal. She was living at the Cottages, near Heavitree Gap, and I used to go and spend a lot of time with her, do her shopping and just be with her. I'd help prepare meals and do all sorts of odd jobs.

Hettie used to love talking to me, telling me all the stories of the old days. About how she'd met Ida Standley, who they'd named Standley Chasm after, when they were out at the Finke River and ran out of food. And about the time she'd been jumping from one rock to another when she discovered a big python under one of the rocks. The rock rolled over and she could feel it sliding on the big python. She took off.

She also used to tell me stories about the countryside around Alice and the way she used to hunt. I remember all those stories very clearly, including stories about the old people at Emily Gap and how they walked through there. How they used to gather there for different ceremonies and how there were certain places where the women couldn't go near the rock paintings. She spoke about all of that.

When she was talking about these sorts of things, Charlie used to be embarrassed and didn't like to listen. He used to get annoyed and say, 'But we're living in different times now, Mum. You've got to get on with it.' I thought he treated his mother harshly, like a lot of kids do. I felt he was lucky to have a mother. I talked to Hettie about my mother and every time we'd get together she'd ask, 'How is your mother?'

Hettie was very strong on maintaining her links with the Aboriginal system and she used to tell me lots of stories about where she came from, who she met with, including white people, and how she related to the land. She had kids to several men. Besides Charlie and Ernie she had other children, and yet she really nurtured me during my holidays up there. Even though I was staying at St John's Hostel I'd often go to her place and sit down and talk with her.

She'd also give me money to buy things, just for doing odd jobs around the house. And she'd go out playing cards with all her friends – mostly Aboriginal women, though there might be one or two whites thrown in among them. They'd gamble for hours and hours, gamble all their money away. She'd often come home with pennies, sixpences, maybe pounds, and she'd give me handfuls of threepences – that was so much money in those days. I'd say, 'I don't want all that, just give me enough for an ice cream or a drink.' In those days ninepence could buy a freshly made orange juice from Harry Sing's Chinese shop: a shilling could buy a huge glass. And they were the best orange drinks you could ever have – freshly made, with ice, even when the temperature was pretty hot, 38 or 40 degrees.

Hettie gave me all this money but she wouldn't give any to her own kids. Ernie and Charlie would be home and she wouldn't give those two any money at all unless they really pestered her for it. She'd say to me, 'Don't give it to those two lazy kids. They're no good!'

While we were on those holidays we'd go out hunting and walking the ranges, just being out. I used to love shooting. Malcolm Bald had rifles and we'd go and get a kangaroo or two. We caught wallabies and kangaroos and brought them back for old Hettie and she'd cook them and we'd have a good feed. One time someone brought back a goanna and she started cooking that. And while we were sitting there with the wood oven going, the tail of this cooking goanna suddenly forced the door open. It was like it was trying to escape. Still alive. It frightened both of us but we got a good laugh while she struggled to get the door closed again.

Hettie also had a network of people who came from everywhere, from the bush, to visit her. They'd come and sit out in the backyard. One of these people, I found out later, was her brother and I used to talk to him a lot. Hettie was the strong matriarch, she bossed everybody around, and this network of hers would bring people from all around Alice Springs to talk to her. They even came from further south, right through to South Australia. One time, coming back on the train from Alice, I had to bring this bush plant, pituri, a mild narcotic, with me. Hettie had sewn it up in this linen bag with 'Mrs Starkey, Port Pirie' addressed on it. The woman met me at the Port Pirie station to get this narcotic. I didn't realise the effect it had on people. That's one of those Aboriginal things – you mix it up with a bit of ash, a certain ash from a particular tree, and chew it and it makes you high.

Another person I met at Alice Springs was Ken Hampton's father, Old Tim Hampton. He was from Borroloola and was related to me in the Aboriginal way. He once had a station called Rosie Creek, between Borroloola and Roper River. He told me, 'During the Depression me and my wife and kids just walked out of the station, left the saddles and everything on the stockrails. Just walked off.' Tim was a Garawa tribesman, although he was on Mara land at Rosie Creek Station. When I met him, Tim was living at Alice Springs and he had his wife there, who they called Mum Hampton. Tim was very kindly towards me every time I saw him because of that Borroloola relationship.

By the time I was fifteen, Malcolm Bald was in charge of the home. He had helped me make contact with my mother and he also wrote a few letters on my behalf, as the head of the home, to the Welfare Department. As it happened, this fellow called Bill Holden and his wife Evelyn, who used to be at Borroloola with the Welfare, and who were now in charge of the Bungalow at Alice Springs, and they were instrumental in bringing my mother down from Borroloola to meet me.

My mum came down to Alice at Christmas time. I had just finished Le Fevre Tech, where I'd got my Intermediate Certificate, and was about to start my apprenticeship. I was still living at St Francis House, but it was arranged for me to go on holidays to meet my mum. When I got to Alice Springs, I knew she would be there, but exactly where and how I was supposed to meet with her was never organised. I was very apprehensive about meeting her for the first time. All those thoughts like, 'Why did you leave me?' were still there. I was angry and confused. I was quick to judge in those days but for once I wasn't sure. I didn't know whether to get angry with her straight away.

After all the treatment that we had, we knew our lives weren't normal. I objected to the sort of treatment that was thrust upon us. I objected to the stream of people who looked after us who each imposed different disciplines on us, and had different ideas on how we should be treated. I hated that, I just hated it. So when I went to meet my mother I was looking forward to leaving school and the home and becoming independent, looking after myself.

In Alice Springs, Boofa Huddlestone and I walked up the street alongside the Stuart Arms Hotel, which is on the corner of Todd Street, the main street in Alice. There was a woman opposite, on the river side of Todd Street, and when I looked at her, I saw she was looking at me.

Boofa and I were halfway across the road when we saw her. We came back to the corner, and she strode across to us. She walked across the road to meet us.

'Where are you from?' she asked.

I said, 'Borroloola.'

And then she said, 'What's your name?'

And I said, 'John Moriarty.'

She said, 'I'm your mother.'

Boofa and I sat down with her right there, on the kerb. We just sat on the ground and started talking. I didn't even hug her. I was carrying years of uncertainties in my mind and I wasn't going to jump in and give her any hugs or anything. When we sat down she touched me, but not for long. She just touched my hand. A very brief touch. I'm sure she got what she wanted out of that very brief touch. It was a very gentle touch.

My mother was slim, fine-boned, very graceful with her movements. She had a very astute mind, she was bright-eyed and she was absolutely clean all the time. She was wearing an old bush dress, an old cotton dress that she'd been given in a Welfare hand-out but she was always immaculate, always polite. She had a lot of grace. When she walked it was with extreme dignity, straight, like an old bush person. You could see the poise. And she was very fit. She had that kind of long, easy stride that meant she could go for days. She must've been in her thirties when I met her, and she still looked very young – nearer twenty-one or twenty-two. Of course when I was fifteen I only looked about twelve or thirteen, because I was slight-boned, very much like her in stature.

When we started talking I didn't even ask her about why I was taken away, what the circumstances were. The first thing she talked about was family. That was good, but at the same time it was sad because she had to tell me that my grandmother was dead. She knew how I felt about my grandmother and how my grandmother felt about me.

We kept talking, then we moved to St John's Hostel, where Boofa and I were staying, and we sat there talking some more. Then she had to go back to the Bungalow. I met her there the next day, and then I kept going backwards and forwards to her. We were there for about three weeks or more, in Alice Springs.

After that first meeting I felt a tremendous amount of warmth coming from my mother. I just used to touch her sometimes, or give her a hug occasionally. She held my hand a couple of times. That's what's stuck in my mind. She'd hold my hand, both hands. And she'd just talk.

I took my mum around to Hettie's place to meet her and we just sat there talking. And she loved that. Old Hettie treated us like guests, both of us. She said, 'You're a good boy, looking after your mother like that.'

And I said, 'No, I'm not looking after her. You are!'

Hettie never forgot my mum and every time I used to see her

she'd ask after her: 'How's your mother going? Is she alright still? You should look after her.'

Hettie was always reinforcing my Aboriginality and she was a good friend. Years later, I was in Melbourne on a visit when I got a phone call saying that she'd died. I just got up and left to go to the funeral. I remember crying like mad.

My mother wasn't able to tell me much about the Aboriginal side of things. Mothers aren't allowed to tell their sons that, it's not their role. They do it only with their nieces and daughters and so on. What they can do is reinforce your family life and your part within the structure; they're just not allowed to talk about male ceremonial roles.

Even so I was really happy to see my mother, to really make a connection, and I felt an inner peace after our meetings. At that stage I wanted to get back to Borroloola, but not to stay. I wanted to go back to see people and to see the place again, but what was uppermost in my mind was my independence and setting myself up for the future. We knew even at that stage that a lot of the people up at Borroloola were being trained on cattle stations to work as stockmen – as ringers, stockmen or fencers. But I always felt that wasn't a life for me. I didn't see a future there.

As it turned out, after my mother went back to Borroloola I didn't see her for twenty years, although I tried to get there many times. It didn't seem so long at the time, and we kept in contact through our letters. What was important for me was that meeting my mother began to complete the jigsaw puzzle; it was the piece I needed to make myself feel whole as an individual and move onwards. As far as my identity was concerned, as a full tribal member, it was the family aspect on which to build. Without it there would always have been lots of question marks.

I realised much later in life that lack of identity was what a lot of the kids that I was brought up with suffered from. They didn't know who their real family was and what their tribal relationships were and what they should've been. It was a huge relief to me to sit with my mum and talk. It allowed me to make my peace with that generation and the family.

Chapter 5

Boy
to
man

At the height of my
soccer-playing career

BACK IN ADELAIDE I STARTED LOOKING FOR A JOB. I ended up putting my name down at a couple of places to be an apprentice fitter and turner. We had been told to aim to do well in life. 'If you have a trade it will always stand you in good stead. You'll never be out of a job. Why don't you be a fitter and turner?'

Wally McArthur, Jim Foster and Charlie Perkins had taken on apprenticeships in fitting and turning so I thought, 'Oh well, that'll do for me as well.' I was accepted straightaway for a job at Birkenhead, at a small workshop rather than a factory. At the home, though, Malcolm Bald said, 'I'm sure you can get a better place to work than that.' His father worked at Osborne Power Station as the leading hand electrician. I put my name down as an apprentice but the intake for that year had already concluded, so I'd missed out. Then I was asked to an interview at North Terrace with a man called Marlowe Kimba, from the Electricity Trust of South Australia (ETSA). He was a very clean-cut man with blue eyes and a fine moustache and we got on very well. He gave me my first real job.

Because I was late with the intake I had to start at Marleston, which was a fair distance from St Francis House, where I was still living. I had to ride a pushbike about fifteen kilometres a day. I'd leave before dark to start work at 7.30 a.m., ride up the Port Road, then head along the South Road and on to the Marleston workshop. I worked there for six months, turning out brass parts, until it was okay for me to be transferred to the Osborne Power Station, closer to the home.

There was one other apprentice from the home already at ETSA. His name was Peter Tilmouth, and he was an apprentice electrical fitter. He was very fair and tall and wasn't easily identifiable as an Aboriginal person, but he did break the ice in some areas. I was a lot darker and more obviously Aboriginal.

At Osborne Power Station there were lots of people who had come back from the Second World War and who had been through all sorts of experiences. I was fascinated by some of the stories they told – about the different peoples and different cultures they'd seen. Some of the men were embittered; some had benefited from travel overseas. As far as the atrocities of the war were concerned, some chose not to talk about them. For others, a young Aboriginal person who was eager to learn made an unthreatening audience. Some of them took me under their wing and started telling me their stories. Others would talk about their adventures but not the tragic aspects of battle.

I enjoyed my apprenticeship, on the whole, and there were only a few testing times. One fellow, his name was Allan Hoffman, didn't like me at all. He had been in the army in the

Second World War and had been a boxer, a pretty good one, too. There was a bit of racism there on his part and one day he had a go at me and started a fight. It began with a bit of a wrestle and I was pretty quick but he was a huge man, he was about thirty or forty kilos heavier than me. He started wrestling me and I wriggled out of his grip, but then he had a swing at me. He got me with one swing. He hit hard, right under the solar plexus. He knew where to hit. I was winded but I had a swing back. I wasn't going to give up easily, because I didn't start it. Eventually we were broken up and the bloke nearly got the sack for it. That all quietened down and most of the time it was little incidents where we had lots of fun.

While I was learning my trade I wasn't having much luck with girls, even though I was starting to notice them. At St Francis about the closest I ever got to one of my first girlfriends was to give her a dinky, a ride on my bike. I sat her on the bar and pedalled the bike off. I can still smell the femaleness of her, the freshness and everything like that. I thought, 'How delicious a girl is.'

A little later, when I was about sixteen, the owner of all the Hoyts theatres throughout Adelaide allowed boys from the home to go to the Saturday matinee at the Semaphore Ozone for free. It used to cost a shilling so we thought free admission was the best thing. On a couple of occasions I arranged to meet this girl in the theatre. It took so much courage just to sit next to her. I think it took three or four sessions. Then this particular day I put my arm around her. I'd scratched the back of the seat for a while first, before I put my arm around her. She must have got sick of all this, the slowness of it all.

I leaned a little bit closer, tried to kiss her and all this sort of stuff and then I thought, 'Oh, I should touch her breasts.' I put my hand under her shirt and felt her singlet. I said to myself, 'Just pull that up there.' The idea was to be bold and do these things – or so I thought from the way the other kids talked. So here I am pulling the singlet up and it kept coming and coming. In the end I realised it was a petticoat. I must have had it about halfway before I gave up.

It was those sorts of disasters, the awkwardness of youth and adolescence that you go through, that put me off girls for a long time. We had been given a facts-of-life talk at the home – a one-and-only-time talk on sexual relationships that was quite informative for me, and was supplemented by what the kids whispered to each other. At the home, as we grew older, they didn't seem particularly restrictive of our activities in this direction. There wasn't much they could do anyway because we were starting to have our own lives in the community.

A few of the boys, like Vince Copley, were much braver with girls. I was in awe of him, how cool he was with girls. I was extremely shy. That was my basic problem.

When we used to go up to Alice Springs, I got keen on some of the girls at St Mary's Hostel, too. I felt a little more at ease with the Aboriginal girls than I did with the white girls. I suppose there was a commonality of upbringing – and I was beginning to be conscious of the white and black situation.

On another occasion there was a girl who used to live on Robin Road, near the home, who I thought I'd love to develop a friendship with. I knew she caught the bus on Hart Street, to go to Port Adelaide Girls' High School. It took me weeks and weeks just to walk with her to the bus stop. I spoke to her once, walked with her once, and then I gave up. I thought, 'Oh, this is too hard. It is too difficult for me to do it.'

I didn't strike up a relationship, much to my regret. I thought she was very nice and I don't think I'm often wrong in picking personalities. I just didn't have the courage to get to that first stage of a relationship, then move on and treat things as normal and do things together. It took a long, long time for me to do that. I suppose I was always worrying about how the girl would feel about me. And rejection was one of those things that had been part of my upbringing. I hated rejection.

I think my fear of rejection was out of all proportion, and I regretted it later. That's why I immersed myself in sport, because I could do that without any hurt or embarrassment and less fear of rejection.

My soccer career began with the Port Thistle Club, next door to the home. When we first arrived at St Francis House, the adjoining property was an open paddock. After a couple of years, the Port Thistle Soccer Club started to use it for a training ground. One day the State Intermediate team was training there, and we sat on the wall and watched them.

We were poor as church mice and had no soccer training to

speak of, nor boots or clothing, but eventually they asked us, 'Do you want to have a game? It'll give us a little extra practice to sharpen our play.'

I was one of the smaller ones of that particular group – I must have been about thirteen, maybe fourteen – but I joined in. We thrashed them. We were all under age, under eighteen, yet we beat this team something like 7, 8 or 10–nil. They couldn't get near us. We were faster and had better ball control. We whisked through their defence and scored goals with ease.

After that game, Port Thistle asked some of the older kids to play for them. The promise of soccer boots was the biggest lure. And we used to play our own games as well. We'd play during the holidays from eight o'clock in the morning, from after breakfast, right through till dark. Sometimes we'd even play in the moonlight, we were so full of energy. All we had to play soccer with was a tennis ball, but we'd play six, seven, eight, ten a side – often in quite confined spaces in the courtyard at the home. That was good fun, learning to control the ball and so on.

About that time, too, I saw Ken Hampton run in the School-boys Championship at Adelaide Oval. He was a great 800-yard runner and in the second half he just powered away. He left his final sprint too late, though, and came second. He was a great athlete but he was never coached properly. I think he could have done really well if he'd been managed properly.

Wally and Jim eventually went over to England to play rugby league. Wally played for the Rochdale Hornets and Jim played for Wigan and Leigh. They were tops. Wally was one of the best in the world and a great all-round athlete. In Sydney, when he was sixteen, he was among the fastest sixteen-year-olds in the world and he was very much sought after as an athlete but, like Ken, he was never managed or coached very well.

I much preferred soccer to Australian Rules or rugby. I always found the cold at Semaphore very hard to cope with and I didn't like having to grab the ball with cold hands. Soccer was a little different. Not being very big myself, I soon discovered that when it came to soccer if you were physically fit and well disciplined, you could hold your own, irrespective of size.

Of course, size is an advantage in certain positions, but speed is an advantage in other positions. I tended to play in the forward line on the wing because I had developed good ball control. With Port Thistle I ended up having a couple of games with the Juniors, then I played with the Intermediate standard and then I ended up playing Senior games, all before I was eighteen. Port Thistle teams were basically people of Scottish descent, very strong on soccer. I liked those people, liked playing with them, but soccer was not a mainstream sport in Australia at the time.

One of the areas where Port Thistle had been training was the corner of a paddock which belonged to the stevedores, where they stabled the horses that were used on the wharves. Eventually Port Thistle amalgamated with Port Adelaide, which was just nearby, and we moved to their field, about a kilometre away. We used to walk across the paddocks to where the Port Adelaide field was. There were still lots of wide open spaces then. After the teams amalgamated, quite a few kids made the State Intermediate team, including Gordon Briscoe and Vince Copley. I didn't make it, though, and that upset me quite a bit. I ended up playing for a number of clubs, including International United. International United was started by a fellow called Drago Bronovic and another man, Branco Phillipi, who was the businessman behind the club. Mr Phillipi had the flashest car I'd ever seen – a huge Chevrolet. His obvious wealth impressed me. I was only seventeen or eighteen at the time but I played with them and it was thrilling, what with the game and the flashy bright red and black uniforms.

United was a bit of a glamour side and we'd all run out with the flashest tracksuits, with an Indian brave embroidered on the back. Of course the big attraction was you got the tracksuit free, plus a jumper that you wore as a bit of a status symbol – it was real state of the art, in bright red, black and white. And the boots, real soccer boots – I thought I had it made. I wasn't getting paid to play at that stage but I was learning my soccer, the discipline. It was almost like doing another apprenticeship.

A little over a year into my apprenticeship, in early 1955, I left the home and went to live with Bruce Holland and his wife Billie and their family as a boarder. Bruce was one of those blokes who frequented the hotel after work, right up until six o'clock; I didn't like him drinking but I liked him as a person and he and his family were always kind to me.

Relishing my new-found independence, I bought my first car. It was a standard eight tourer, a 1940 model, and it was on blocks more than it was on the road. I paid 165 pounds for it – and I lost a lot of money on it. I suppose that's one of the things you go through in life. It really taught me a few things.

Between working and soccer, I was beginning to discover what it meant to be an Aboriginal in the wider white society. We were never allowed to be wandering around at night time, for example. We were well known in the district as 'the boys from the home'. Because we looked different, we made an easy target and we were often told, 'You kids get home because you're not allowed out here.' Effectively, it was the community's way of saying, 'We know who you are and where you're supposed to be.' Some were quite good about it, others were not quite so good, and we learned to move in the circles of least resistance.

One Sunday afternoon Ken Hampton and I were walking down St Vincent Street in Port Adelaide, and Ken was with his girlfriend, a white girl, when a policeman stopped us and sent us home. He was quite within his rights because Ken was breaking the law by consorting with a white woman. This upset us, of course, but it was the law at the time.

For me, one of the really embarrassing ways of trying to meet girls was going to dances. They used to have dances at the Port Adelaide Town Hall and if you wanted to be part of the social life of Port Adelaide you had to go. I only went to two.

At the first one the girls were all on one side and the boys were on the other side. I was with my mates, who were all about the same age, seventeen or eighteen, but there was a range of age groups right up to mid-twenties. When the music started, it was like a starting gun had gone off, and the boys thundered across to the other side to ask the girl of their choice to dance. A couple of girls I asked didn't want to dance with me. They just said no and that really put me back. I don't remember asking a third.

A few weeks later I thought, 'I'll give it another go. Maybe it's just me – I may not be up to the standard of dress or whatever.' Of course, the possibility of it being about race was present in my mind all the time. I said to myself, 'I wonder if it's because I'm black.' There was still a lot of stigma in those days about being an Aborigine and I ended up thinking that was part of it. I got knocked back one, two, three times – and the only time I had a dance was the progressive dance, the barn dance, where they change partners all the time and you swing around and that's it, on to the next one. So you're not dancing with any one person, you're just a link in the chain.

After that, I thought, 'Well, I'm not going there to be embarrassed, asking someone for a dance only to be humiliated.' And I gave those dances away. They put me back in my social life for a long, long time.

And then I found out that once you become known a little, you are more accepted in all sorts of areas, including with girlfriends. While I was playing soccer, the girls were sort of attracted to the game – and to me. I said to myself, 'Well, this is not bad. This is the way to go!' I took a few girls out who were supporters of International United. I remember there were a couple of Dutch girls and I became friendly with one of them. The better soccer I played, the more popular I became.

That was very important to me in those days, although I really had yet to be accepted socially. I wanted to be accepted as an individual rather than as a soccer player, but I suppose the girl bit still made me feel good.

After playing a season with United I moved to Birkalla, and then I went back to Port Adelaide.

Meanwhile, through my work at Osborne Power Station, I became friends with Mick O'Malley. Mick had been born in Glasgow, Scotland, although his parents were from Ireland. He was a fitter's mate, as they were called, and one of the country's top soccer players; he'd played left back for Australia. He'd also done a stint in Malaya with the British Army. Then he came to Australia and married into a soccer-mad family. Mick was the team coach for Port Adelaide but he still took the time to give me advice on soccer.

He said, 'If you want to play soccer you have to be physically fit.'

So I said, 'Alright, I'm willing to learn and play the best soccer. Would you coach me?'

So after work he'd take me out on the field and make me run. He was a pretty hard taskmaster. When I was out of breath, tired, fatigued, he'd say, 'Right, you've had your rest. Now do this.'

And he'd get me running more. I'd be right at the end of my tether and he'd say, 'Give it a little bit more.'

He coached me right through my soccer career and I always respected him. I confided in Mick about many aspects of my life. We became firm friends and I still consider him a dear friend today.

In 1958 I was chosen to play for the State youth team. John Lindquist coached the youth team and about seventy-five per cent of the players ended up playing in the State Senior team. He put a lot of time and energy into soccer and I have a great deal of admiration for him.

When the State youth team played Port Augusta, it was 41 degrees and we beat them 6–0. It was a real lesson playing in that terribly dry heat. I was offered a glass of beer after the game to quench my thirst, but being a non-drinker in those days I couldn't even stomach that. I remember saying, 'I'd drink anything now, I'm that thirsty', but I spat out my first mouthful, I just couldn't swallow it. And I've always disliked it since. At that time, I'd seen Aboriginal alcoholics in cities living with no soul or spirituality, with no sense of being Aboriginal, it seemed to me – and it made me feel that we should never allow ourselves to become like that, certainly not me.

During the time I was with the youth team we had a very rigorous training program which had us constantly trying to beat our own times. John Lindquist was very much a physical fitness man and a couple of those players were gasping by the end of a training session. Each session we had to time ourselves. It was an honour system and those that put the most effort into those training sessions were the ones who really benefited and made it to the senior level.

A couple of the players were quite skilled but didn't have the determination and stamina to reach a high peak of fitness. I was always gauging myself and pushing myself to reach my goals, and I was naturally fit. I loved most sports but soccer was the one that really took my passion. It was an international game and through it I made a number of friends who we called 'New Australians'. They were Polish, they were German, they were Yugoslavs and Italians.

What I found really interesting was that the better I played soccer, the easier it became to be more socially mobile.

I also felt a lot better about mixing with girls; I felt a lot more natural, and people were starting to accept me because they liked me as an individual. At the time I probably had an unrealistic view of what constituted a relationship. Like any teenager, I suppose, I had sex on my mind a lot of the time.

People talked about things like condoms but I never bought any. I thought, 'Oh, gee, I couldn't get myself into a shop to buy one.' They were sold at chemist shops and there was a bit of a myth going around that a couple of girls got pregnant because the chemist at Semaphore used to put pinholes in the condoms he sold. I guess someone was just peddling those stories around, but it certainly frightened me off. Not that I was doing anything to need condoms – I wanted to, but it just didn't happen.

My first attempt at sex was when I was beginning to mature

as a soccer player. I was at the Semaphore sideshows, where I'd met this Aboriginal girl. We were kissing and everything and I thought, 'I'll try and have sex with her.' I tried. I thought that near her belly button, near where the pubic hairline starts, was round about where you're supposed to aim for. I can still picture that disastrous attempt. I embarrassed myself, as well as embarrassing her – and she was a willing partner!

After that, I said to myself, 'I have plenty of time.' I made up my mind that I wasn't going to get married until I was about twenty-eight. And I decided that was quite realistic with my attitude towards life. I felt I had so much to do.

By the time I was twenty, I'd finished my apprenticeship. After I finished, though, I felt a little disgruntled that I hadn't reached any great milestone. I was still at the power station, doing the same sort of work after five years. I wasn't getting a buzz out of it anymore.

Soccer was my overriding passion. Then in 1960 I was selected to play with the South Australian State soccer team; I was asked to represent the State. I didn't know it at the time, but this meant that the president of the South Australian Soccer Association had had to seek permission from the Protector of Aborigines for me to travel interstate to represent South Australia. Technically, the association would have been breaking the law if it took me, an Aborigine, to Perth for my first game.

For the trip to Western Australia we flew in a DC-6B. It was my first plane trip. It took six and a quarter hours to fly there and it was very exciting. When darkness fell I thought the engine was on fire, because the manifolds were glowing red. I was so concerned that I actually told the flight attendant. She must have had a good laugh at me.

I played two games over in Perth. The position I played was right wing, and I had fun, absolute fun, in both games. I was bursting to play well. With my physical fitness, I was sharp, and my mental agility was on a par. I had two extremely good games. I recall stepping over the ball a few times, back-heeling the ball. I was getting the ball on the run in front of me after passes backwards from my team-mates and cutting in towards the goals.

We scored twice in the first game. I was very adventurous in that game and I had a good feel for the ball immediately. I scored once and hit the crossbar on another occasion, after a bit of play that I was really happy with. As the ball was bouncing, I flicked it over to one side, over the head of an opposition player as he turned, then I flicked it back over the other side and as it came down I volleyed it and it hit the crossbar. I was on fire.

Immediately after the game the press wanted to interview me. I was taken to the radio station, but I asked for a couple of the other players to come with me because I didn't think it was fair to single me out. I thought the interview went badly; it didn't exactly flow because I was so shy, but the next day I had a good write-up in the Perth paper.

The media liked my style, my play, and I was buoyed by the

publicity. It didn't make me feel like a star, though. I always thought, 'The next game is the important one. You must keep building for what's ahead of you.' I never looked back or rested on any glories. I always learned from the previous game, and went over my mistakes. I constantly asked myself, 'Can I do this thing better? Can I improve on that?'

I have to admit I've made some glaring mistakes in my time, but I did build a style where I could control a ball. I could move with a ball from a standing position over the first few yards very quickly and could pass accurately most times. The second game I played was a very good game, too, and it secured my place in the team for the next few years.

In Perth an English journalist was covering the games on behalf of the UK football pools. His name was Bernard Moss and he saw me play in my first two games, then at the Australian Championships in Melbourne in June. He suggested I play soccer in England and said he'd put my name forward to Arsenal, Tottenham Hotspur and Everton. He actually came to Adelaide to talk to me.

Those were exciting times for me. I loved the game and I wanted to go over to England to play – and to experience the sort of life described to me by people who'd played there. They said, 'Well, you should do it.' But in the end it came down to a lack of resources to go – I needed money, a job when I got there and, I thought, some expression of interest before I went to the other side of the world.

It was when I was representing South Australia at the Australian Championships in Melbourne, in June 1960, that I found out about needing permission from the Protector of Aborigines to travel. I thought, 'This is an insult, having to seek permission from someone I've never met. Who is this person who has control over my life?' Being an independent-minded person, and having just turned twenty-two, I thought I was representing the State in soccer in my own right, which was as an Australian. I thought, 'This is an indignity that no-one in Australia should suffer.'

At the Australian Championships, South Australia did very well, but New South Wales was the strongest team. It had five Austrian international players in the team plus Johnny Barr, who was one of the best Australian players, and the Kitching brothers, who were strong, natural, raw-boned players. When we played New South Wales I had all these fellows chasing me. I had a lot of pace and good control of the ball; I could change directions and kick with either foot, and I could roll with the tackles. People could bump you but they'd never throw you off balance because you'd roll with it, just step over and you'd hardly come into contact with the opponent.

I was able to do that against New South Wales that day – I'd get by one, get by two and then they'd get frustrated and literally rugby tackle me. We were getting free kick after free kick, but I thought, 'If this is the way professional players play I won't have a bar of it. I'll just show them how to play real soccer.' I came off pretty bruised and sore after that game. That was my baptism of fire.

The game ended in a draw. We were winning up until the very end, when their overall strength levelled us out. From then on, though, our team had a reputation as the dark horse in the competition. I thoroughly enjoyed those games because I was allowed to play at the very highest level in the country and I was matching wits with the best – not only skills but brains as well – and I revelled in that.

I laughed inside, I was bubbling inside every time I got the ball. For me there was sheer enjoyment in what I did. I had a lot of determination to win and to break in at this level so I was keen to do my best. I played and had lucky breaks. Every game I'd learn something new. I'd do new tricks, at a quicker pace, with players who were at the same level.

In those days I was also playing Aussie Rules with the ICI football team, with Boofa, Malcolm Cooper and Richard Bray, just to loosen up with a little bit of extra running. I used to have a lot of fun with those fellows at ICI; they weren't a bad bunch. And Boofa, Malcolm and Richard went on to become star Aussie Rules footballers with Port Adelaide.

I was bursting with fitness, bursting with life and I just wanted to enjoy life to its fullest. Mind you, I prepared for it very well because I was in bed early as a rule and up early. I never drank, I never considered smoking. I was a quiet personality off the field and one way I expressed myself was with a little bit of flamboyance on the soccer field.

Back in Adelaide, on the Monday night after the Australian Championships, Bob Telfer, the chairman of the selectors, said to me, 'Look, have you heard that one of the reasons for the championships was to select a team from Australia to tour South-East Asia?' Then he said, 'The good news is that you were one of the first selected, to play as a centre forward or as a winger. The bad news is that Australia has been disqualified from international competition because New South Wales is fielding the Austrian internationals.' FIFA (Fédération Internationale de Football Association) had banned Australia because these Austrian internationals were not cleared. New South Wales's refusal to back down effectively kept Australian teams banned from international competition for some eighteen months, to the best of my knowledge.

None of this changed the fact that I'd been picked to represent my country. I was on top of the world. I really felt I'd earned my place, and I was walking on air. Of course, not getting to play was upsetting, but I was also still seething about needing permission to play soccer interstate. In fact, that was one of the things that brought me to the Aboriginal rights issues. And it did so at the beginning of a time of great activity.

Back at Ethelton Primary School, a boy named Jim Sinclair had sat next to me for about two years. He ended up going to a different school but we'd stayed friends. He always had a strong sense of injustice, even at a young age. He often said to me, 'Look, we should be doing something in Aboriginal affairs.' His father, Jim Sinclair Snr, also happened to work at Osborne Power Station. He'd sidled up to me one day and confided that when he'd been working on the land, he'd eaten kangaroo. (At the time eating kangaroo was considered to be one of the indicators of how uncivilised Aborigines were.) Jim's father made a point of saying to me, 'Don't be afraid to speak out.' The Sinclairs were humble people, but they got me thinking that a lot of people wanted a better deal for Aborigines.

It was in that same year, 1960, that I first met Dr Charles Duguid, who was famous for his involvement with the Pitjantjatjara people at Ernabella, in South Australia. He was a surgeon trained in Aberdeen, with a broad Scottish accent, a very strong and likeable individual – and also keen on soccer. We hit it off very well. Dr Duguid was already involved in the Aborigines' Advancement League, most of whose members were older people, and he approached me to join the organisation. A lot of the people there I had a ton of respect for – people like Gordon Birt and his wife Jean, Dr Duguid and a few others.

In the end I chose not to join the Aborigines' Advancement League. In South Australian politics, Don Dunstan was also active in Aboriginal rights at the time, and I was impressed by his determination to abolish the exemption card that Aborigines needed to travel freely – an issue I felt very strongly about. Don was also already talking about land rights, although it was barely acknowledged on the political agenda at the time. With Jim Sinclair, Don Dunstan, Charlie Perkins and a couple of others, like the people I was then boarding with, Bill and Jean Huckel, I started taking petitions around. Dunstan spurred us on, and we gained a lot of support, in the form of signatures on petitions, that were presented in the State Parliament.

Unfortunately, Don Dunstan was not typical of the Labor Party at the time. Union representatives at a national level were very set in areas like Aboriginal rights. It took a lot of coaxing to get these unions to support the Aboriginal cause. At the time I was experiencing the consequences of this first-hand. As a fitter and turner, I was a member of the Amalgamated Engineers' Union, which was one of the strongest left-wing unions. Although some people supported our struggle, when it came to the crunch the union wouldn't support me when I asked for equal pay. I was at the Osborne Power Station, doing the same work – and yet I wasn't getting paid the 'dirt money' allowance that I was entitled to receive. A few of the members in those workshops even complained that I was getting as much as them, so my pay was actually cut back in a couple of instances. I'm sure that wouldn't be tolerated now.

At the start, in the Labor Party in South Australia, it was only Don Dunstan who had the charisma and fortitude to get up and speak out about Aboriginal issues. It wasn't considered the right thing to do in those times. Aborigines were still sniggered at, kept in isolation out on reserves, and forbidden to mix with the greater population. Don Dunstan, to his credit, took up the issue and he became very popular with Aborigines for it.

So all of a sudden I was extremely busy – in the soccer world, with my job, with politics – and I still wanted to travel overseas, maybe even play soccer in England. If I could have got up to Borroloola I would have, but I still felt as if my mum would be there forever. I felt I would be around forever, too. (I'm slowly starting to realise that life's not quite like that, but only in the last couple of years.)

Another friend I made in the sixties was a fellow named Elon Percival Champion. He liked to be called Champ. He and his wife, Elva, had no kids and I used to go with them down to the Coorong (a large saltwater lake system near Adelaide), where they had a basic shack. We used to fish and go netting; we went shooting, boating and waterskiing. Champ was an independent type. He was a builder and he also did a bit of travelling out-back, including to the Territory. When I was with him I met and mixed with Aboriginal people and he always encouraged me to continue with that.

People like Champ and Hettie Perkins were encouraging me in a very subtle way. They'd always ask: 'How's your mother?' 'Have you heard from her?' 'What's going on up there?' Hettie used to make me feel guilty that I couldn't get up there and I'd say, 'Yeah, I'll get up there, I'll get up there.' It was a long way in those days, and I didn't have a vehicle. Well, I did, but I couldn't drive very far in that old car.

Chapter 6

Widening horizons

My first trip overseas, here with travelling companions at the Parthenon, Athens

Soon after I had represented South Australia and been picked to play for Australia, Adelaide's best team, Juventus, approached me and asked if I wanted to play with them. The first person I talked to about it was Mick O'Malley, my coach at Port Adelaide. Mick said, 'If I was you, son' – that's the way he used to talk to me – 'If I was you, son, I'd grab it with both hands.'

After playing with Port Adelaide, which was a very Australian team, I was quite daunted by the prospect of going to Juventus, which was an Italian-backed team. At that time, Italians living in Australia were encountering a lot of animosity left over from the Second World War: they were derided as wogs and dagoes, and when I joined the club all these thoughts were going through my mind. Mick O'Malley just said to me, 'Juventus, great club. If you want to play good soccer, you must get with the best clubs.'

Every time I'd played against Juventus, it had always been a tussle. They had some tough players, like Fulvio Pagani who, as the left back, was the man I'd had marking me on most occasions. He also played for the State, and he played for Australia. I wondered what it would be like to play with him.

Anyway, after talking to Mick and weighing up all the pros and cons, I moved across to Juventus in 1961. They were very quick to seek out talent, and they always sought out players who'd fit in with their culture. Once you were in with Juventus you stayed with them and they looked after you. As long as you played your soccer well and fitted in with their culture, everything went well. I did just that.

In total I had represented the State in seventeen games. They were very enjoyable games, too. I think the most games others had played at that time was about fourteen or fifteen, so I thought I was going pretty well.

Going to Juventus showed me the way the Australian people were changing, how people of different nationalities were settling in this country and gradually gaining more status within the community. I also discovered that there was life outside of Australia – mainly from the 'New Australians' that I met, including people like Mick O'Malley. I don't like using the term 'New Australians', but I use it here in the context that these people educated me and I felt no discrimination from them at all. I felt like a free person – a person without restrictions.

If anything, that feeling accentuated my reaction to the attitude towards Aborigines in the wider community. With a lot of the articles in the paper, it was always 'part-Aboriginal player, John Moriarty'. The fans used to call me Johnny Moriarty and they still call me Johnny today. They've got good memories, some of those soccer fans. But I was always Aboriginal to the rest of the society.

All these things – and possibly my brashness when I was younger – motivated me to tackle the issues head-on. With Laurie Bryan, a concerned white businessman, and Malcolm Cooper, who had been in the home at Semaphore, I established the Aborigines Progress Association. It was considered a very radical organisation at that time. We took on the harder issues and made a lot of criticisms where we felt they had to be made. Laurie was white and very much involved with the Labor Party but I don't think I realised at the time how staunch a supporter of the Aboriginal cause he was. He always told me stories about how his father had undersold his skills. His father was a very good tailor in Broken Hill but he'd never really achieved his full potential. And I think this predisposed Laurie to support those on the bottom of the heap.

Also at that time a number of people, including Dr Duguid and Gordon Bryant, who was Labor MP for the electorate of Wills in Melbourne and a strong proponent of Aboriginal rights, were pushing for a national body. The Federal Council for the Advancement of Aborigines and Torres Strait Islanders (FCAATSI) was established in 1961. It was a non-government body made up of Aborigines and non-Aborigines from around Australia and, as a founder of the Aborigines Progress Association, I was invited to participate. From then on, every Easter representatives of the Aboriginal community travelled to and from Canberra to have meetings on Aboriginal issues, and I thought, 'This is the way to go.'

For the first time, this meant issues could be tackled at a national level instead of by individual States, which all had different laws for Aborigines. This was also when the fight for the referendum to give Aborigines equality at a national level began. But that was a long hard row to hoe; we fought and fought for that for years.

The chairman of FCAATSI was Joe McGinness, an Aboriginal fellow born in the Northern Territory. He was a Kungarakun from near Daly River. A tall person with a lot of presence, he was slow-talking, which belied a very sharp wit. Some Aboriginal people didn't appreciate him, but most did. Along with a few other key people, including myself, he travelled the country for years fighting for Aboriginal rights.

We had meetings in and around Adelaide, in Melbourne, Sydney and Canberra, and the momentum was being developed to have this referendum. The wharfies' union, teachers' federations and politicians of both major parties were all beginning to speak out about gaining equal rights for Aborigines. We had a lot of publicity in those early days, and people began to take up the cause of Aboriginal rights, particularly the 'New Australians'. Non-English-speaking migrants were widely discriminated against and they could readily identify with our circumstances.

In the early days what I found was that many people in the Aboriginal movement had no idea of their tribal backgrounds and their identity. Yet many still felt strongly that they should be doing something to gain equal rights. Their dispossession, the injustices they'd suffered and the problems they had were quite different to the problems that I had. In many cases they were a lot worse. Many of these people had lived in the white community, on the fringes of cities, or on reserves, and they did not have the freedom of movement I had. Restrictions were all-pervading in their lives – like policemen stopping them, arresting them and their families. A lot of those people drank, too. Getting drunk seemed to be one way of drowning their memories and sadness, albeit temporarily. Often it was an escape for them.

Technically, I was still a ward of the state. However, I didn't apply for an exemption card because I thought it was degrading. I had registered to vote even though, according to the law, I was not a citizen of the country that I and my predecessors had been born in for hundreds, if not thousands, of generations. However, my being involved with soccer and being fairly well known within the Adelaide community meant I was sheltered from much of the day-to-day persecution and legalities inflicted on other Aborigines.

This was the lot of people like Winnie Branson, who was involved with us at the Aborigines Progress Association and was a staunch fighter for equality. Winnie was born on Point Pearce reserve on South Australia's Yorke Peninsula. Her forebears had been forced to go there from their land around Port Lincoln and the nearby Poonindie Mission. Winnie's brother was Vince Copley, who had been with us in the home. Winnie's mother,

Katie Copley, instilled in her a strong commitment to Aboriginal equality.

Winnie had a good mind, had her feet firmly on the ground and fought very hard. Through her I was able to connect with the Point Pearce community. However, like too many Aborigines, she died an early death and she is buried in West Terrace cemetery, in Adelaide.

Winnie's aunt was Mary Williams. Although Auntie Mary was not as consistent as Winnie in her fight for Aboriginal rights, she could come into a meeting, say a few words and completely tip the meeting on its ear, just leave it in a shambles. She did this on many occasions. She often clashed with Malcolm Cooper in those Progress Association days and he would get so frustrated with her. She'd say a few words and they'd be at each other, trying to come to some sort of balance in the proceedings. But Malcolm would end up screaming at her, she'd be screaming at him and we'd have to pull it all back from there. She had a habit of doing that.

Laurie Bryan couldn't cope with her either. I was okay. I found she was antagonistic towards people who'd stand up to her in a particular way. That would really make her get on her hind legs and say, 'Right, I'll fix this fella.' I suppose I tended to disarm her and we got on very well. I thought her whole family was very intelligent and had just not had the opportunities they should have had; they could have gone a long way.

Identity was one thing that I was able to lend some of the dispossessed people I came across. Coming from the Northern

Territory I had links back there, although some of them were quite tenuous at that stage. Still, I could tell them things like 'This is my name and this is my tribe'.

Winnie would say, 'We've lost a lot of our past, I only know my tribe and the background we come from.' She could tell me only a few words of her Aboriginal language; like most Aboriginal languages, much of it had been lost. (Out in the bush these languages still survive, but in the cities and heavily settled areas they have almost gone.) Yet there was that commonality. We were able to unite Aborigines on a number of issues and one of those was persecution. We did not have equality, we had discriminatory laws – no matter where we came from in Australia. So we were able to unite under the one banner to get rid of the exemption card and start pushing for land rights.

Sport proved to be one of the most effective ways of uniting people. In South Australia Winnie Branson and I started the Nungas Football Club, an all-Aboriginal Aussie Rules club, to get Aborigines involved and united. Winnie was very keen on that. Mostly it was Point Pearce people who came into the football club but we ended up getting some Point McLeay people, as well as some Territory players. The football team had an occasional game with the police. We'd trounce the police, often in the first quarter. I think there was a bit of a payback there going on with some of those players.

The Aborigines Progress Association was working on the sporting front, the legal front and land rights, as well as equality in general. Issues were popping up all over the place. One of the big issues was the legal status of Aborigines.

In Adelaide, the police and Aborigines were virtually at war — every day, every night. The hotels were not very good places for coexistence. Before the referendum, only Aborigines with an exemption card could go and drink in hotels. Even though I didn't drink myself, I thought it was degrading to need an exemption card just to be able to drink.

Also, because when you got the card you became a legal entity within the Australian system, you had to get declarations from welfare officers, police and other authorities stating that you had achieved a standard of living equal to that of a white person and should now be legally treated as such. No other race was subjected to this. It also meant forfeiting your Aboriginal identity.

I thought, 'If all of that is what I have to do to get the card, I don't want it.' I fought very hard to get rid of the card so that we could become normal citizens — be Australian — yet still hold onto our culture and identity.

The meetings in Canberra with FCAATSI were really invigorating. We'd talk about what was happening in our State and in other States and see exactly where we were progressing. We found out that Victoria was pretty well integrated but there was still a long way to go everywhere. The fight for Aboriginal rights in South Australia was being seen as the model for campaigns in other States. People like Don Dunstan were credited with a lot of that. He was taking up the issue in the State Parliament while we rallied to particular causes and showed our presence with demonstrations on the steps of the House and so on.

Many of the Aborigines who joined in those demonstrations were alcoholics, people that were downtrodden and had been badly treated for years and years. They had been treated as second-class citizens for so long that they had begun to feel, think and act like second-class citizens.

At several of the demonstrations there was a fellow from Point Pearce called Doc Wanganeen, who had been a brilliant foot-baller in his day. He'd had an operation that had left parts missing from his neck and he was a heavy drinker, but he had a very strong sense of justice and he always stayed sober for these rallies.

One night, though, he just couldn't help himself: he hit the drink before this particular demonstration at State Parliament. Don Dunstan was speaking in the House, and when the Opposition was speaking against Dunstan's reforms, old Doc suddenly erupted from the public gallery, shouting, 'You're just a mob of racists. I hope you cop your lot.'

Of course, this was unheard of at that time but Doc was a pretty wily sort of character and once he'd had his say he took off. By the time the stewards scrambled up there to clear the rabble-rouser from the House, he was already gone. Everyone was sitting there open-mouthed, just watching.

That was probably the first time that the whites in the House, the politicians, were directly confronted by Aborigines. It was not a very pleasant mood either, and I'm sure that set them thinking. That seemed to mark the beginning of the process of change.

While Don Dunstan was taking up these issues legislatively, we coordinated our fight in the press and elsewhere with our meetings and the other strategies we developed. We also started travelling to mission settlements. At Nepabunna Mission, in the Flinders Ranges, a Mr and Mrs Hathaway were in charge, and we'd had complaints from Aborigines there that they were virtually holding the community to ransom. The only shop would be closed for days at a time because dogs were barking at night; tribal languages weren't allowed to be spoken; and the last time an initiation ceremony had been held in the area was in 1947.

I drove up there after a soccer match. My car broke down just outside of Port Pirie and I hitchhiked a lift to Port Augusta, where I met up with Malcolm and Aileen Cooper, Lois O'Donoghue (now Lowitja O'Donoghue), Laurie Bryan and Bert Clark, and then we drove up to Nepabunna and met with the Hathaways.

We were ushered away from the Aboriginal people, discouraged from speaking with them, and Mrs Hathaway sat us down in her living room. She gave us a cup of tea each and a biscuit. Mr Hathaway, who was missing an arm, seemed like a reasonable person once you started talking to him. He freely gave his views. Then Mrs Hathaway said, 'You know what the trouble is here in Nepabunna?'

I was sitting on the edge of my chair, holding onto my cup and saucer, wide-eyed like the rest of the group, waiting for some profound comment.

She said, very dramatically, 'S-I-N. Sin!'

I sat back and thought, 'Oh, how can I compete with this?'

I got the impression she was running things with an iron fist. And she regarded everything Aboriginal as a sin against God. The local people hated her.

Obviously we ended up meeting with some of them. Some we realised were not even allowed on the reserve. They were at Copley, about fifty kilometres away, waiting for a chance to get back to meet with their relations.

In 1963, with my friend Champ, I tried to get back to see my mother and my relations. We arranged to travel up to Borroloola in his Chrysler Royal, a utility with a canopy on the back. We went in May, which is supposed to be the start of the dry season up north.

We drove from Adelaide to Alice Springs, then up to Daly Waters on the Stuart Highway. Daly Waters is 380 kilometres west of Borroloola, and from there it's dirt road all the way. After about sixty kilometres the road degenerated into a series of mud patches. We tried to get through, but in the end we had to give up.

We headed up to Darwin to give the road a week or so to dry out. On the way back down to Adelaide we tried it again but there had been more rains and the same thing happened. That put paid to that visit to Borroloola. I'd got to within 320 kilometres of home, the closest I'd been since I was taken away twenty years before.

Back in Adelaide, I started thinking of heading overseas. The

Italians I was playing with at Juventus were a real fraternity; I'm still friends with many of them today. There were a few hotheads among them but we found a great common passion in soccer. The Italian people kept saying, 'You should go and play in Italy.' Someone suggested, 'You should go to Genoa.' A couple of Yugoslavs were saying, 'Go and play in Yugoslavia.' And of course the English sportswriter Bernard Moss had earlier encouraged me to play with a number of English clubs.

I finally decided to go overseas in October 1963. For the soccer season, I should have gone earlier. By the time I arrived it was mid-season and it was impossible to break into it. I travelled with John Finlay, who was a fitter and turner at the power station with me; his nickname was Turk. He had red hair and freckles. We went with Turk's brother, who was an albino nicknamed Louie – and Louie's mate Tony Smith came too. He was an olive-skinned fellow with dark brown hair.

We left Adelaide on 10 October 1963, and travelled to Melbourne on the train. From there we boarded a Greek ship, the *Patris*, to Sydney, sailed to Wellington in New Zealand, back to Brisbane, round Cape York and across to Colombo. We were supposed to call into Singapore on the way, but there was a cholera outbreak at the time.

Colombo was my first real experience of a truly foreign country. It was absolutely filthy. The streets were filthy, there was rubbish piled up everywhere, and I was very thankful that I lived in Australia, which was still pristine and without a lot of people. The poverty in Colombo was mind-shattering for me.

The next port we docked at was Aden, then we travelled up through the Suez Canal and arrived in Piraeus on Christmas Eve. We used the boat like a hotel for three days, travelling to nearby places in Greece, then caught the ferry across to Brindisi in Italy and hitchhiked to Rome, Florence and Venice. By the time we got up to the north of Italy it was too cold to hitchhike. There was snow everywhere.

We caught a train to Munich, bought a Volkswagen and travelled together right through Europe. We ended up going to more than thirty countries and principalities, from the Sahara right through to Scandinavia. We went all over the British Isles, from John o' Groats to Land's End – it was foggy, we couldn't see anything. Then we went over to Ireland. When we went to Killarney, I saw a sign saying 'Moriarty' over a chemist's shop. I just walked in out of the blue and asked, 'Are you a relation of John Moriarty who went out to Australia, to the Northern Territory?'

They said 'No, we're not your relations. Try somewhere else.'

I went to a few places, including Tralee (where, I would later discover, my father's family came from). I felt good at Tralee on that very first visit. I don't know why but I said to myself, 'There's something about this place.'

I looked around but I couldn't find any Moriartys. We were tearing through Ireland but we spent a night at Tralee. The thing is, while I was there I was looking for a connection, even then.

One of my big regrets of that time is that I didn't settle with a soccer club. I just trained in Sweden. The truth is, I was really enjoying myself. I was twenty-six and what really stuck out for me was meeting and mixing with people. I had always been told I was very narrow in outlook; that trip overseas broadened my outlook considerably.

I was particularly struck by the attitude of the English. They enjoyed life, they enjoyed people for what they were. If you were a likeable person, they didn't discriminate on colour – at least the people I met didn't. In Australia discrimination was enshrined in law. A lot of the time it was probably me as well, being self-conscious or overly sensitive, but in England I really noticed the difference.

After nine months overseas, two things made me decide to return to Australia. First, I was called back to Australia to play in the Australian Soccer Championships for Juventus. The club wanted to fly me back at their expense. And by then I had also decided that I should give it a go at university in Adelaide. I had come to realise that was a stepping stone to a better job, and to being recognised in Australian society.

Subconsciously, I may have decided to go to university before I went overseas. Although I was a semi-professional soccer player, I still had to work for a living. I thought, 'Well, if I can get into a team over there that would pay me, I could do my university studies.' That was one of my intentions. Then seeing the cold over there, the winters, I realised it would have been very difficult for me. What I should have done was perhaps play in Italy. They had drier grounds, warmer summers. Of course it gets very cold, but not as cold as in the long playing seasons of England.

Even so I regretted not playing soccer in England, or not giving it a go there. I lived with that for the rest of my life. I'll never know if I'd have made it.

I arrived back in Adelaide on 11 June 1964, and went straight from the airport to a Juventus home game, at Hanson Reserve. When I walked onto the ground the crowd forgot the game for a moment and turned to greet me. I'll never forget that welcome. People still mention that moment to me.

When I got back I also found a letter waiting for me from a woman named Miss E. M. (Merle) Griffin, who lived in Burwood, Melbourne. Accompanying the letter were a number of photographs. The letter said they were pictures of me, as a small child, taken back at Borroloola.

It turned out that on board the ship I'd taken to Europe there had been a woman from Melbourne who was on her way to Istanbul for an International Red Cross convention. Merle belonged to the same Red Cross group in Melbourne – and this woman had told her all about her shipboard meeting with a man called John Moriarty from the Northern Territory who had moved to Adelaide.

In the early 1940s Merle had been working at the Postmaster General's office in Melbourne. Out of interest she had organised a trip to Borroloola with two friends, and had written a couple of articles about it for the magazine *Walkabout*. She journeyed up through the centre, through Brunette Downs, Anthony Lagoon, up that way to Borroloola and came back through Mount Isa and down the East Coast. She told me that she travelled in the mail truck and while she was at Borroloola she spent a number of days with Ruth Heathcock, the local nurse, and her husband, Sergeant Ted Heathcock, a policeman.

While she was there, Merle spent a lot of time with my mother and she became quite attached to her. She and my mother travelled everywhere in a dug-out canoe and walked along the riverbanks finding bush tucker. My mother helped her a tremendous amount. They got on extremely well – and I guess Merle must have liked me as well because she kept telling stories about me, and she wrote about me in *Walkabout*.

Merle had found my address through Gordon Birt, an ex-policeman who had been at Borroloola and was quite friendly with Ted Heathcock, the policeman Merle had stayed with all those years ago. They had both retired from the Northern Territory police and were now living in Adelaide. Merle had written to Ruth Heathcock asking if she knew of my whereabouts and the Heathcocks had contacted Gordon Birt.

Gordon had made a point of visiting me when I was at St Francis House in my final year of high school. He used to invite Boofa Huddlestone and me to his home in Glenelg. The story goes that the first time we went there they served us a meal and Gordon's wife Jean kept serving food and serving food until she thought we were going to burst, but we just kept going and ate them out of house and home. Since then, I'd gotten to know

Gordon and his family well. Jean was an Aboriginal lady from Point McLeay reserve, and they had a son called John.

Gordon liked Borroloola and I'm pretty sure he had a relationship with my mother before he got married. He was a very nice man and I liked him very much. He was of Irish descent, an Australian of Irish descent. Gordon was a very strong proponent of Aboriginal rights, even though he was a policeman, and he often got into trouble for not treating Aborigines according to the strict letter of the law. He once told me he'd had to arrest Nemarluk, an Aboriginal outlaw who was the nemesis of the police in the Northern Territory during the late thirties and early forties. They chased him, arrested him and locked him up but he always got out of jail and disappeared again. He was a real bush Aborigine who could survive on the land, and he eluded the police until Gordon arrested him.

Gordon put Nemarluk on horseback, as was his duty, but instead of hobbling him in chains he made an agreement. He said, 'Come back and face the courts, face the police and I won't put the chains on.' Nemarluk agreed and they went on horseback from the Timber Creek area right through to Katherine, camping and talking along the way. Gordon said Nemarluk was a fine upstanding person. He said, 'I was arresting him as a person who committed crimes against the state' – making Nemarluk one of our very first political prisoners. Gordon also knew of Merle Griffin's visit up there – he had a great memory for detail, like a lot of Irish people.

When Merle wrote to me she was certain that I was the child

she'd known at Borroloola. Her letter talked about meeting my mother and me, and her travels around Borroloola and her photographs.

I wrote back to her, saying, 'I've received your letter and I'd like to meet you.'

It turned out that Merle had dozens of these magnificent black and white photographs of my family, all taken around Borroloola. She had all the negatives in individual brown envelopes and each envelope had a number on it and a caption. Some of those photos, and she'd taken quite a number in the region, featured me. She'd also taken a lot of camp shots and scenes of the surrounding country. There were pictures of different people in the camps, doing everyday things like boiling a billy can and traditional cooking. One photograph showed the dug-out canoe with all of us in it, all of our family, even the dogs. The canoe looks pretty full. You'd wonder how people could survive, paddling across all those waterways in such delicately balanced dug-out canoes.

Although I have no recollection of the photos being taken, they brought back strong images of how life was up there. I seemed to be part of it just by looking at and identifying with each shot. There was Old Donegan, whom I met years later – he was still strong although he was a very old man by then. And of course my mum; I couldn't mistake her profile and her face. Since my meeting with her ten years before she always looked the same to me, even when she was very young.

Apparently Merle had also met my father, but she didn't say

very much about him. She said, 'I met a John Moriarty in a vehicle that was bogged in sand just outside Borroloola.'

I asked her, 'What he was like? Did you take a photo?'

She said, 'I took a photo of the vehicle in the sand but I didn't take a photo of the people in the background.' She didn't volunteer any other information about him because she only met him very briefly. She had just been chatting with people that were bogged in the sand – people going one way, while she was headed in the other direction.

Looking at the photos I thought what an organised lady she was. She knew every person in those photos, and she pointed out my mother. I felt good about seeing those photos. It's one of those other connecting things, as if all the pieces of a puzzle are being put together and they fit.

Merle and I ended up becoming very close friends. Over the years, she's given me a lot of moral support – and even ended up giving me a small interest-free loan during a critical financial period. She just volunteered it – I would never have asked.

We had a great relationship. Merle was a remarkable lady. When she was in her early eighties she did a trek to the Himalayas and she headed up the mountains, walking. Then a few years later she travelled to Norfolk Island and she showed me photographs of the track she'd followed. She walked all around the island. She was that sort of person.

Sometimes I stayed with her at her unit in a retirement village, just to catch up with her. We'd eat, have a chat, then I'd sleep on a mattress on the floor, and leave the next day.

She eventually gave me all the negatives she had, and she got quite a number of the photographs developed to give to me. When she was downsizing her belongings, she gave me some of her chairs that were over 150 years old and a table, as well as a few other items of furniture that I liked and have held onto.

Merle was very dear to me but she had lots of people that she helped. I was just one. Her sister had had a child out of wedlock, and she looked after her niece for years. Merle and I remained close until she died at the age of ninety-two from complications after she had a fall at home and hit her head.

In 1964, when I got back from overseas, I went to work at General Motors, first as a maintenance fitter at Woodville, then at the new Elizabeth plant installing press lines. I was living in a flat in Semaphore, playing for Juventus and training hard to get back into the State team.

The next year, 1965, I started doing my matriculation at Saltash College, to prepare for entry to university. That year turned out to be quite a momentous one for me. During a Juventus game at Hindmarsh Oval, I was given a pass to the right wing. It was out in front, and I made an attempt to get it, but the goalkeeper came out and I met him at full speed. He dived just below my knee and my body moved forward over him and bent my left knee back. That ripped one cartilage completely off; the one on the other side was half off.

I didn't realise how much damage had been done until I had surgery quite some weeks later. They didn't do it with an arthroscope in those days. I was cut open, they opened the knee out and just cut things off here and there. I had the two cartilages put in a jar which I kept on my mantlepiece for a while. I was in a rehabilitation program for months. I played two more games after that before my knee gave out again. That was the end of soccer.

Although I was on a different path with my career, soccer was my sport and I just wanted to play. I was absolutely devastated. I tried very hard to do some more running and strengthening. I had a doctor look at it. He said, 'Just try and build it up with strength training and weights.' I had weights for years, but it didn't do any good. It was one of those things that was meant to be, but I still sometimes find it hard to accept.

On the positive side, though, the end of my soccer meant I had more time for politics and other pursuits.

Chapter 7

Forging ahead

Studying for matriculation at Saltash College,
Adelaide, to gain entry to Flinders University

GOING TO UNIVERSITY WAS ALMOST BEYOND the comprehension of a lot of the peers I'd done my apprenticeship with. Most of my friends were getting married but I was still thinking, 'I need to do a few things before that.' Education was one of those things.

When I finally enrolled at Flinders University, in 1966, one of the nicest things that happened was that the registrar, Frank Mitchell, said to me, 'We haven't got any Aborigines here. I'd like to welcome you.' I was very thrilled to be welcomed there. Frank Mitchell was a lovely man and I felt good about Flinders from then on.

Actually, to the best of my knowledge, I was the first Aborigine in South Australian history to go to university. At twenty-eight, I was older than the general run of students and there were some derogatory comments about my age and being black. One fellow even said, 'What's he doing here? He's an Aborigine – he shouldn't be here. He should be back with his own mob, back on the reserves.'

I don't recall that person going on to do anything special in life, but I always remember his derogatory comments. It was times like that I used to think, 'Oh well, what's the good of having stand-up fights with people like that?' I just resolved to avoid those sort of people. I didn't cop those comments a lot, just here and there – enough to remind me that things were still not the way they should be. And this spurred me on as well.

In fact one of the fellows I went to university with dropped in to see me years later. He said he was still embarrassed about something his father had said to my face. I'd long since forgotten about it but this fellow hadn't. His father had said: 'Oh, it's good that this Aborigine is at university, even though his intellectual capacity is not as good as ours. At least this primitive person is here to try and better himself.'

There were a lot of good people at university, though, and people like Champ were very encouraging, too. When I went to university he said, 'That's the best thing you can do.' Champ's father had made his living chopping wood. Champ hadn't been to university and he wanted to know all about it: about the social life, and about how I was coping with everything. It was a very steep learning curve. I'd been a worker in a factory, where work was geared around very strict times, like morning 'smoko'. The factory whistle would blow and you had your ten-minute smoko; you'd down tools. In the Amalgamated Engineers' Union, which I'd joined when I started my apprenticeship, the unionists said, 'You must do this, you must have your smoko, you must have your time.' I thought you always had to finish the job you were doing, like we'd been told in the home, but the unionists said no. 'We've got to have our smoko and our lunch breaks and all this.'

At university, decisions and discipline came from within the individual. You'd have lecture times, of course, and tutorials, but study was up to you. I found I had to work very late, even though I had always been an early riser. I was an early-to-bed person for years and years, and when I went to university I switched to staying up late. I just ended up getting less sleep because I couldn't sleep in. I still can't.

I got an Aboriginal Scholarship (ABSCHOL) in my first year at university to supplement my own savings and I also got some help from the Aboriginal Education Foundation. ABSCHOL was funded by student union contributions from all over Australia and was very meagre in those days.

In my second year I got forty-two dollars and seventeen cents a fortnight from a new Commonwealth Scholarship for Aborigines. I lived well on that – and I was quite happy to do so. To help make ends meet, I had a meal occasionally with Millie Glenn, who I grew up with at Mulgoa and who was now in Adelaide. She used to wash my clothes occasionally and I'd do odd jobs for her in return.

At the time the ABSCHOL people were among the few elements of white society with a bit of a conscience on Aboriginal matters. Ironically, though, in those days more white people were involved than there are now. Whites are not generally accepted, or invited to participate in Aboriginal affairs, and I think that's a real shame, because I think such complex issues need talented and qualified people, regardless of race. Self-help is essential but if, for instance, you don't have enough Aboriginal doctors you should be able to ask for help from white doctors; you should be able to do that with all professions.

At university it took quite a while to discipline my mind to cope with setting a timetable for my courses, lectures, when I had to come up with assignments and so on. It took a bit of adjustment to work to that system, but in the end I enjoyed it. And in the end it was good for me because it showed me the life and culture and opportunities of another section of the community in Australia.

At Flinders I did Australian history, English and colonial history, geography and politics. I had wanted to go to Adelaide University to study anthropology, to learn more about Aboriginality, but I'm glad I didn't. My course ended up broadening my outlook a lot more than anthropology would have done.

I probably should have done economics as well. Some years later, I met Dr Nugget Coombs in Canberra and he said, 'What's your degree?'

I said, 'Bachelor of Arts.'

He replied, 'You should have done Economics.'

He wasn't brash, just pragmatic in approach. He was always against dogmatism. He was very likeable and I learned a lot from him.

When I started at Flinders I imagined it would be a hotbed of radicals. Some of the lecturers and some of the mature-age students thought they were radical; they thought they would really create something in the world. The sixties seemed like heady times when we look back on them now, but I didn't think they were so significant at the time. I was more or less just going along the path that I wanted to go, as were a lot of other people.

My professor in geography, Murray McCaskill, was very encouraging, and I came to really enjoy the subject. The professor of politics was Don Corbett, and he was a Canadian fellow. I found him a nice person but I found pure politics a bit dry. I was more interested in creating the change, but obviously you have to learn about the existing system if you want to make any effective changes.

I went to university a bit bright-eyed and bushy-tailed, and I had to come back to basics to get on to complete my degree. It ended up taking me five years to complete a three-year degree, but there were some major distractions for me.

The first two years of my university course coincided with the lead-up to the 1967 constitutional referendum. Called by the Federal Government, the referendum was to decide whether to give Aboriginals citizenship and voting rights by virtue of having them counted on the census. If passed, it would also give the Federal Government, rather than the State Governments, much of the responsibility for Aboriginal affairs.

While all this was going on, Don Dunstan was pushing his reforms in the State Parliament and we were organising demonstrations and talking to the media and trying to get our message across. At one of our demonstrations the usual staunch crew was there – Doc Wanganeen and his mob from Point Pearce were holding placards and making sure people noticed us – when Lois O'Donoghue came by. She would eventually become chairperson of the Aboriginal and Torres Strait Islander Commission, and here she was immaculately dressed in this suit with gloves. She walked by and exclaimed, 'How undignified!' And off she went towards King William Street.

Not long after that, she was given a job with the South Australian Department of Aboriginal Affairs. At that time very few Aborigines were employed by the government – and none of them were people with reputations as rabble-rousers or radicals.

Many people, myself included, devoted a lot of time and energy to the referendum, and I had to keep increasingly flexible hours. By then, I was heavily involved with the Aborigines Progress Association, as both treasurer and vice-president. Malcolm Cooper, one of the boys from the home, was the president all the time I was at university, and we got on well. Laurie Bryan was the secretary.

The Progress Association also had a lot of the other St Francis House lads. We'd bring in people like Boofa Huddlestone and Jerry Hill at times, and to a lesser extent Winnie Branson's brother, Vince Copley. Vince had become a farmer by then. He'd married Brenda Thomas, a farmer's daughter, and he worked on the family farm.

Vince used to come over for FCAATSI meetings in Canberra with us, with Jerry and sometimes Boofa.

But it was Malcolm Cooper, Faith Bandler, the poet Kath Walker (later known as Oodgeroo Noonuccal), and a handful of others who were involved in a series of meetings with Sir Robert Menzies during which the referendum was planned and instigated.

One time Malcolm came back from Canberra and recounted how Kath Walker had been at this meeting with the Prime Minister in his private office at Parliament House. She was being her usual fiery self, saying, 'We don't want the white people doing this, the white people doing that. We're sick of the white man's poison, how it's degraded Aboriginal people.'

She pretty well covered all the things the whites were guilty of since 1788. Eventually the Prime Minister said, 'Look, now that we've finished all our business, you're welcome to have a drink.'

He asked what Faith Bandler wanted and Faith was offered a drink.

Malcolm Cooper had just learned to appreciate good Scotch whisky and said, 'Yes, I'll have a Scotch whisky.' And he was duly given a fine Scotch.

Then the Prime Minister turned to Kath Walker and said, 'I know you don't like the white man's poison and all the other things that belong to the white man so I won't offer you a drink.'

Kath enjoyed her little taste of alcohol and, quick as a flash, she said, 'Oh look, this is one of the things that I'm just learning to appreciate from the white man. I've tried it a bit. I'll try it again.'

And she drank with the Prime Minister.

In the lead-up to the referendum, Aboriginal politics was becoming increasingly high-profile in the press and was constantly being brought to the attention of white people. I attended many meetings and spoke at some, including to the press, so I started to get a great deal of publicity for the comments I made. That public profile helped me in a number of ways. First of all it gave me a great deal of confidence in getting up and speaking to people. It wasn't that difficult, I suppose, as far as subject matter was concerned, because all I was speaking of was the Aboriginal experience. What I was still learning, though, was how to convince the public to help the Aboriginal people and how to give them a greater understanding of our problems. That was crucial to securing a yes vote.

I was always shy, and I still don't push myself forward. I also tend to push issues and principles for the greater good, rather than for myself, and I see more good in people than bad. I'm an optimist, to a fault I'm told. In politics this can be interpreted as naivety but that's part of my make-up and I'm sure I'll never change.

Like a lot of shy people – and lots of Aborigines are naturally shy – I'd rather be in the background than in the foreground. Even in my soccer days I'd allow my expression on the field, in my game, to speak for itself, rather than going about being the loudest on the ground. I always found that those people who called out, talked and blamed others for their mistakes on the field were not taking responsibility or achieving the things they should have as part of a team.

I was telling Aboriginal people that they should identify with their culture, but at the time it was not as important as the major hurdles, like gaining equality. I knew we shouldn't lose our culture but at that time Aborigines had many things impinging on their lives that affected them daily.

During my years at Flinders University and the referendum campaign, I was fortunate in meeting a white man called John Scanlan. Through his work at the Department of Labour and National Service, John had been in touch with the Aborigines Progress Association about the idea of embarking on a program to bring Aboriginal people into the workforce. John and I ended up developing that together. During my university vacations I began to work with the department to help develop and implement the programs we initiated.

At that time the department had responsibility not only for South Australia but also for the Northern Territory, and it encountered a lot of political flak over the employment conditions of Aborigines in the Territory. The Department of Labour was embroiled in the landmark fight for equal pay on pastoral properties that resulted in the Wave Hill walk-off, when Aboriginal stockmen simply refused to work and left the Wave Hill station.

As a result of this action, the decision was made in 1966 to grant Aborigines employment on equal terms within the pastoral industry, although the policy was not implemented until Christmas 1968.

The day of the referendum arrived. In theory, Aborigines were not supposed to vote unless they had an exemption. I didn't have an exemption but I still registered to vote the day I turned twenty-one, and I've voted in every election since. I thought everyone should have that democratic right and I fought very hard for it.

The referendum was passed by a ninety-one per cent majority, the highest in any Australian referendum.

Around the time the referendum was won, there was a great deal going on in the United States with Malcolm X, Martin Luther King and the marches in the South. The civil rights marches in America had the sympathy of most Australians, as far as I could tell. However, when it came to the Aboriginal situation, it was a different story. Australians had first to come to terms with the reality that many whites had family histories that were very closely entwined with Aborigines. Although there had been a lot of intermarriage, there is still some stigma attached to having Aboriginal blood. As one Aboriginal friend in Victoria, Elizabeth Hoffman, fairly accurately described the situation: 'There are more whites in Australia with Aboriginal blood than Aborigines with white blood.' The consequence was that no-one wanted to give Aborigines an inch. Even though it was now their right to be citizens of this country, with equal rights, Aborigines had to eke reforms out of white Australians.

I still think of this as an indictment of white Australians. They looked at the civil rights movement in America more sympathetically than they did the Aboriginal cause here. The situation of the American Indians is more like ours. People in America like to think they have a good relationship with Indian people but when it comes to returning Indian lands, they begrudge every little bit. It's the same here.

Although a lot has changed now (particularly with the younger people, who tend to relate to Asians and Aborigines a lot more easily), I still find that people like to have someone underneath them on the social scale – whether it's Aborigines, Vietnamese, people of a different culture or people who look different physically. Aborigines fall into that category all the time.

At university I got engaged to a white girl called Diana Rogers. She was blonde and blue-eyed. I got on very well with her, extremely well – in fact, I was madly in love with her. I got on well with her family too, yet I was the one who caused the split, because I thought the black/white thing might not work out.

I confided in Charlie Perkins about it. He had married a white girl and he said to me, 'Yeah, you're right mate. Marry an Aboriginal woman, you won't have that problem.'

I took his advice. I said, 'Yeah, I suppose so.' And we split up.

After we split, Diana went over to England with a girlfriend of hers, travelling via South Africa. Then I made contact with her when I was over there and wanted to put it all back together, but it was too late.

Forging ahead

In the late sixties and early seventies the first national Aboriginal sports carnivals came into existence, and these had the effect of further unifying Aborigines. It all started with an Aussie Rules game that I had organised between a South Australian team and a Victorian Aborigines' Advancement League team in 1969.

For that first game Laurie Bryan and I collected money from students and, with the help of a contribution from ABSCHOL, we raised 320 dollars to hire a bus to go from Adelaide to Melbourne. The bus was a 32-seater with seats that were just leather straps strung across metal frames. At the pick-up place we found out that we didn't have enough players so we drove the bus around to the Carrington Hotel, just behind the Adelaide police headquarters. We pulled up just as the pub was closing. A few people were there and I asked, 'Who wants a game of footy?'

And a couple of young fellas piped up, 'Ah, we do.'

'All right, hop in the bus.'

They didn't know we were going to Melbourne, but we bundled them in the bus. Then a couple of people that were already in the bus said, 'Oh, he's a good footballer over there. We'll get him to hop in the bus, too.'

Some of those fellas woke up the next day to a hangover – and the surprise discovery that they were in Melbourne. It was a bit of a new twist to the 'blackbirding' trade.

One of our new 'players' was a fellow from the Northern Territory I knew. His family came from Borroloola and his name was Tommy Muir.

He said, 'What's goin' on?'

I said, 'Oh, look, hurry up. Get your gear on. We're playing in a minute.'

And he said, 'Whaddaya mean?'

And I said, 'You're here to play footy. You know, you agreed to play footy.'

He didn't have any gear and he realised he was in another city but he still got ready to play football. We borrowed some gear and played a couple of people short. And we had our first inter-state Aussie Rules game.

Victoria thrashed us, needless to say, but everyone had a great time. The sense of unity at grassroots level that arose from that game was a revolution.

The following year we held a carnival in Adelaide, and Western Australia got involved. The next carnival was in the Northern Territory, in Darwin, and teams from the Northern Territory, South Australia, Western Australia, Victoria and Tasmania participated.

Both the Tasmanian and the Victorian teams were made up of Aborigines who were very fair in colour – and the Territory Aborigines, most of them tribal blokes, said, 'Who are these people here? We're playing white people.'

I said, 'Oh, no. Their parents are Aboriginal people but they've been mixing with the white people for a long time and have lost their culture and their language and things like that.'

That's when the mob from the Territory felt really sorry for them. The tribal people went, 'Oh, you can't lose the law, you can't lose that system.'

They had a lot of sympathy for them and that further unified the movement.

Through our organisations – and through sport – we were extending our Aboriginal identity, our sense of community and our sense of belonging as a group of people. We were very successful in beginning that process through that carnival.

All this time, though, I kept thinking, 'There has to be a greater force behind Aboriginal people than just sport and sharing external factors that bring us together, like unequal treatment and discrimination.' Those things are strong but I thought there should also be a basis for making people feel good, getting the satisfying feeling that can make people better human beings. I was thinking about the expression of Aboriginal identity through song and dance and art.

I've always felt strongly Aboriginal, right from when I was a kid. Although I was taken away and denied a lot of my heritage and my culture while I was growing up, and when I was older I should have been doing a lot more to reclaim my Aboriginality, it was still there as a driving force under the surface. For me, it is that inner fabric you build on to do all the other things, to keep the end goal in your sights, even when it is only achievable over a decade or two or longer. It keeps you going while you're still striving for things.

A lot of people find what they're striving for, perhaps on a single issue, and then withdraw from the movement after that. That's part of the problem in Aboriginal affairs – a lot of people get what they want, then they drop out of it. That's where some of our people are missing out because others use the Aboriginal movement for their own ends. For many, many years I've fought to fix up the politics and to strengthen people's spirituality, so they can be an integral part not only of the Aboriginal world but also of the wider Australian community. People should feel good about being part of it – with their own identities clear, precise and strong – so they can move on and their kids can move on the same way.

Also at this time I became aware of the fact that some of the white people used Aborigines for their own benefit. To my mind, academics were often prominent in that category. They gained PhDs and a lot of standing when they wrote about Aborigines, but their concern was more for their careers than for the well-being of the people they were studying. To me that was just another way of exploiting Aborigines.

There were some people, though, who were genuinely beginning to see the plight of Aborigines and the value of Aboriginal culture and were giving it support in Adelaide. Foremost among them were Dr Duguid of the Aborigines' Advancement League, Dr Harry Penny, Dr Helen Caldicott, Chris Hurford (who became the Federal Member for Adelaide in later years) and, of course, Don Dunstan.

Max Hart was one academic who was involved with tribal Aboriginal society, as well as some urban Aboriginal communities. He was with a teaching institution which later became part of the University of South Australia. Max accumulated a large collection of Aboriginal art that was later given to the university. I was suspicious of Max at first but in the end our paths came closer and closer as we worked towards the same goal. Max recorded a great deal of Aboriginal culture and he tried to keep out of the politics of Aboriginal issues, but what he produced was of a wholly political nature anyway. He said to us, 'Look, I'll do what I'm doing as long as it's okay with you.'

He was involved in collecting art from Aboriginal communities and teaching about it, with the aid of Aboriginal artists, which got our message across anyway. He was saying, in a very rudimentary way, 'This is one of the things that is important.'

It was early times and Max had great vision, greater than I did in those days, of where Aboriginal art should go. As time went on, I saw the value of that more and more.

The really ironic thing is that white Australians first discovered Aboriginal culture through overseas eyes. Australians are very slow in adopting anything that is homegrown. Everything has to be appreciated by people from overseas saying, 'Oh, you've got something great here.'

And we go, 'Oh, have we?'

Aboriginal art had to be re-imported back to us, when it had been exported in the first place. White Australians had to be shown it was there. It's not just Aboriginal things, though. In many areas we Australians often seem unable to see the best in ourselves.

I finally graduated from university in 1970. By then university had become a means to an end, not an end in itself. I made quite a few friends but I didn't really join in the social life of the university. I was never a drinker or a smoker, and I was never part of the in-crowd. I don't consider myself a follower of other people; I have my own ideals and principles. But there were people there I looked up to or who had qualities that I admired, and a few became valuable role models.

When I got my university degree, I became the first Aboriginal graduate in South Australia. Part of my reason for wanting a degree was to gain acceptance in society, despite my colour. I was proved right about that – because once I achieved a degree, and had BA on the end of my name, people really treated me differently. I was no different in myself, except maybe I'd learned a few more things on the way.

My involvement with the Department of Labour and National Service during my university vacations almost guaranteed me a job there at the end of my course. I believed very strongly at that time, and I still do today, that employment is a very important aspect of Aboriginal affairs – employment particularly in mainstream society, 'proper' jobs in other words.

What this means is that Aborigines must have the appropriate qualifications to get the best jobs. Up until the mid-sixties, Aborigines were in menial jobs that were very poorly paid, with few qualification requirements. So when concessions were made by the Commonwealth to assist employers who had Aborigines on their payroll it was a major step forward. This enabled Aborigines to move into areas where they'd never been employed before and to move up the ladder within the companies that employed them.

It's worth noting here that, at this time, the government departments, both State and Federal, had almost no Aborigines working for them. You could count them on one hand. But our program made it an embarrassing thing for governments not to have Aborigines on their payroll, particularly in areas such as Aboriginal Affairs. Obviously, Aboriginal people could understand their own people's conditions and problems far better than white people, and their employment by government departments constituted a major step forward.

When I left university I moved into a full-time position with the Department of Labour and National Service, in the Aboriginal Employment Unit, which was established specifically to devise Aboriginal programs. The idea was to employ Aboriginal people within the department as vocational officers, and I was the first to be placed in the position of vocational officer, at Class 5 level, although we still faced detractors within the department. However, in time, the pressure became such that they were often overridden – and, to his credit, the regional director of the department, Billy Sharpe, took on the issue and had the program adopted throughout the department. This was the forerunner to the similar programs now in place in many Commonwealth Departments.

I take my hat off to John Scanlan. He had a lot of barriers to overcome, and I believe he fought very hard to become one of the pioneers in the public service. I'm sure he was bypassed because of his stance with Aborigines; it affected his promotion up the ladder within the department. I respect him to this day, and consider him a friend – in fact, I still call him 'boss'.

John continued to work in Adelaide to develop the vocational officer system and mainstream employment opportunities for Aborigines until his retirement in the early 1990s. John is still well respected in Aboriginal circles in South Australia.

At the end of 1970 I made another attempt to get back to Borroloola. I'd just finished university and, for the first time in my life, I had a reasonably decent car. It was a '63 EJ Holden, a two-tone cream and turquoise one.

While I was at university I'd befriended a fellow from America, an anthropologist called Jim Pierson. He was doing a study of Aboriginal people in Adelaide, and I decided to take him up to Borroloola. He was very keen.

We spent a couple of days in Alice Springs on the way, staying with Hettie Perkins. As usual, one of her first comments was, 'How's your mother?'

I said, 'I'm going to see her.'

She said, 'Oh, it's good you're going to do that.'

We headed on towards Tennant Creek, Jim and I, and it was *very* hot. We struck a few heavy thunderstorms going through and I was starting to worry whether we would get there. We decided to keep to the bitumen road wherever we could. I knew there was a bitumen road heading north towards Borroloola through Brunette Downs from the Mount Isa Road (now the Barkly Highway).

The road to Brunette Downs might have been bitumen but it was still very narrow and it was so hot. I could only afford retread tyres in those days and just before we got to Brunette Downs homestead we blew a tyre – the whole tread came off. We ended up driving into Brunette Downs to buy a tyre. I was appalled that I had to pay twenty-three dollars for a new one. That tyre took a lot of my money – money I'd set aside for food and petrol.

Continuing from Brunette Downs we came across a vehicle we thought was broken down. There were a lot of Aboriginal blokes there and I asked them, 'What's the trouble?'

They said, 'Petrol.'

So I gave them some petrol and I was expecting them to give me some money for it but they just took the petrol and drove off, leaving me with even less money. I started hoping that when we got to Borroloola I could conserve my money by catching a lot of our own food.

We struggled on through Anthony Lagoon, Mallapunyah, Balbirini. We were getting closer. And then, by the middle of the afternoon, just before Christmas 1970, we were there. Back in my country. It was twenty-eight years since I'd been taken away.

I felt a little bit of apprehension, but not very much – more excitement, I think. I knew my grandmother was gone but my mother was still there. Borrolooloa was a beat-up old town, worse than places like the railway sidings at Oodnadatta and Marree and some of those Aboriginal camps outside of Alice Springs I used to go to, but I liked the countryside. I felt at home immediately.

The Mulgoa climate had extreme frost on occasions, as well as the warm showers of the summer thunderstorms; then there'd been a lot of misty rain at Mt Wilson and I had some good feelings about that. Adelaide had short, cold winters and hot, dry summers. But up north it was different, the air was different.

And the river was good. I saw the McArthur River and I knew I was born along its banks. There were all these things I wanted to connect with my childhood and my family, including my father.

I drove past the hotel and asked a few people about my mother. I asked for Kathleen, and they said, 'Who are you?'

I said, 'I'm her son.'

They said, 'Yeah, her camp's over there. You can camp over there, next to where the old hotel used to be.'

Because Jim was a whitefella I thought that instead of going to camp with my Aboriginal family immediately we'd camp a bit closer to the town – which was little more than a hotel, a shop, a dispensary, the welfare centre, the government centre and a post office. There wasn't very much there, but then that's Borroloola. I can camp anywhere in Borroloola. Jim was white and American but I was an Aboriginal from that area, which meant I was still part of that Aboriginal system. I felt quite confident being in my own country.

Forging ahead

I met my mother, sat with her and found a deep sense of security not just from being back at Borroloola with my mother but from the way she talked. She always called me 'my son'. Every time I talked to her she'd say, 'Yes, my son. My son, can you do this? My son, what did you do today?' She obviously felt good about me being home.

Willy O'Keefe was always with her – my mother's husband, my stepfather – and he was a really nice, lovely person. He was always kind, always considerate, he never said a nasty word and we got on very well. We did until his death, twenty-five years later.

My mother was still a very active woman then. She was very close to me while I was there and I also spent a lot of time with Amalina, my mother's sister in the Aboriginal way. Amalina's son, Peter Butcher, had been at St Francis House; he had been taken as well. Amalina's sister, Dulcie, was there, too. She was married to Arthur Mawson, a white man who owned Spring Creek Station. They had a heap of beautiful kids. I spent time with all these relations – even Old Donegan, who was in his nineties.

I also attended a few corroborees. They were very frequent in those days. There was no television then and people were still living a very traditional lifestyle.

I met Old Tim, my Aboriginal grandfather, and he took charge. The family systems were still intact, the kinship system ruled and people still had obligations they had to meet. My mother was a very integral part of that. Old Tim was our big boss; he must have been in his late seventies.

Old Tim and my uncle, Musso (who was in Darwin at the time), had strict, rigid control over the people. They meted out punishment, they controlled the community. Food was shared, people were living long lives and the population of Borroloola was still very small. The Aboriginal people still lived out on the stations, still lived on traditional lands or near traditional lands and they came into Borroloola for very special ceremonies. They came in from as far away as Numbulwar, in Arnhem Land, and even from over the Queensland border on occasions.

It was good coming back to that system. I felt totally confident that my mother would live forever, I'd live forever, and that I could come back any time and fit in – which I still do now. I thought the system was good, yet I had a different life down in Adelaide; I was very conscious that I had to make a living.

My people up there at Borroloola said, 'When are you coming home? We want our children to be taught things, have good schooling like you, to learn about the whitefella ways and know about their system.'

They didn't want anyone interfering with the Aboriginal system. They said quite clearly and quite categorically, 'It's our country, our system. We don't want anyone else teaching Aboriginal law but us.'

Jim and I intended to stay for a long time, but we also wanted to drive on to Darwin. As it turned out we were there for a week, sitting with the old people, hunting with them, digging in the mud for turtles and lily roots and all those sorts of things.

We walked around the country a lot. I couldn't drive much,

except on the bitumen, so we walked to a lot of places just around Borroloola. It was a very significant area for me anyway, for tribal life. I was able to learn some of the legends of that country and the dances that belong to people from different areas. I discovered that certain people have more rights to certain land than you have, and that in other areas you can have more rights than other people. The people we were with showed us some of that country. When Jim was there they just showed him around, although he also learned a great deal. He took a great deal of notice of what was being done because of his anthropological studies of Aboriginal tribal life.

I have no biological brothers and sisters, not from my mother's side anyway. I'm not sure about my father but I doubt it, certainly not in Borroloola. Not many people talked about my father at that time. Once I started asking questions, they'd say, 'Yeah, we know him,' but they wouldn't talk very much about him.

We ended up being at Old Tim's camp nearly every day, and in the end we shifted camp closer to him. That's where Jim had his nightmare.

Jim's fear of snakes was extreme – something I didn't realise until we were out hunting one day.

I'd said, 'We need a feed. Tim needs a feed.'

Every time I went out for a feed I'd get something for the old people. That's what I'd often done for people like Hettie Perkins. As long as I can remember, I'd always known that if you catch something, you bring something back for the mob and the old people. They share it with you. So I said, 'I'll go and get a kangaroo or turkey.'

I shot a bush turkey and showed it to Jim, to teach him a bit of bush life as well, because he was a really lovely bloke – we're still good friends. We walked along a bit further and there were a few heavy showers. It was the beginning of the wet season and there were these huge pools of water alongside the road. It was really hot and steamy.

Poor old Jim had shorts on and he looked very tropical; he was just about expiring with the humidity. Coming up from Adelaide and being from California, he couldn't cope with the humidity, not very well anyway.

I thought, 'He's a bit thirsty.' So I said, 'Come and get a drink in these waters.'

He said, 'But that's muddy water.'

I said, 'No, it's real sweet water. Good drink.'

So we went down to this pool on the side of the road. The road was built up a little bit, and we got down there to drink. I gave him a cup. I drank straight from the pool. As I stood up I could see this little head poking up a few feet from us in the water and I thought, 'Oh, looks like a turtle.'

I didn't tell Jim until he'd finished drinking; then I said, 'Oh, I just saw a turtle there.' Next we looked down right at our feet and this thing was swirling around. You could see the movement of the mud from the bottom.

I said, 'Oh, looks like a snake, Jim.' I knew he was scared of snakes, but I didn't realise quite how much.

Just as I said 'It's a snake', this thing leapt between us, from the water. We were only standing two feet apart on this rock and this thing went straight between us. I jumped. I got quite a fright, but Jim really took off. He jumped out of his thongs and ran. But he'd only taken a couple of steps and his feet hurt. So he came back, put his thongs on again, then took off again up the road!

I'm there laughing and calling, 'It's all right, Jim – it's only a water goanna!'

He didn't take very kindly to that.

I missed catching that goanna because he disappeared through a drain under the road into a huge lagoon. Not long after that I saw this snake on the road.

I asked, 'Have you seen these snakes before?'

He said, 'No.'

I said, 'You ever seen the poison fangs?'

He said, 'No.'

I grabbed my rifle so I could show him. I didn't go very close, but the snake was watching us. While you look at a snake, it normally stays still. This one wasn't a king brown – a king brown would've been gone: after the initial advance, eye contact, he'd be off. This one stayed there, so I said, 'I'll shoot him. When he dies, I'll show you his fangs.'

I was a good shot in those days, and I aimed a shot behind his neck, making sure the bullet ricocheted off the road to hit him. There was just a bit of skin left connecting his head and his body.

I gave Jim another drink of water and then, when I thought the snake was dead, I got a couple of sticks and said, 'Here Jim, I'll show you the poisonous fangs.'

I had to drag him almost physically to see it. I said 'You alright?'

He said, 'Yeah, yeah.'

I said, 'Look, come down here, he's dead. Look, he's not moving.'

So I got one stick and put it on the back of his neck to hold the head so I could open the mouth up to show Jim. As soon as I touched the snake with the stick, it had a nervous reaction and its head moved. I pulled my stick back, then I put it back on and said, 'Jim, look, this is the poison fang here.' I was just scooping the fang out to show him. 'Jim?' When there was no reply, I looked around. He wasn't beside me, he was 100 metres down the road in the car!

And even that wasn't the end of Jim's ordeal. We got back to the camp that night and were told, 'We've got this corroboree – a big dance tonight.' On the way there, the river was up from the rains, and we had to wade across just as it was getting dark. That was all right and we went to the corroboree – dancing and everything. It was a great night. Being back at one of these ceremonies with all the pieces fitting together, I was feeling really good.

On the way back, it was completely dark. Now you get the occasional crocodile in that river and as I started wading back Jim was alongside me, wearing shorts. Sticks and other floating objects were drifting past. Next thing I knew, something bumped Jim's leg, something drifting by in the river, and he leapt up, landing on my back. He was twice my size and I had to carry him across!

That night we were camped near Old Tim, as usual – we were just in sleeping bags on the ground. Early in the morning I heard this *huge* scream. It was Jim. That frightened the hell out of me. I didn't know what was going on. I jumped out of bed and there Jim was in his pyjamas in the moonlight. He was fighting his way out of his sleeping bag. Then he started running. He immediately tripped on this little anthill at quite a pace, barefoot – and when he hit the ground I landed on him and tried to pin him down, because he was really screaming. He was in terror.

I held him down, and shouted, 'Jim, Jim! It's me, John, I'm your friend. Calm down.'

He's six feet three inches tall this fella, I'm only five-eight, and I'm holding him down, wrestling him until he came to his senses. The day with the water goanna, the snake and the river, and I suppose the corroboree, must've been way too much for him. And it all culminated in this huge nightmare. It was about snakes.

Jim almost completely lifted the toenail off his big toe when he hit that anthill. There I was in the torchlight, scooping lumps of anthill out from underneath. Early the next morning I took him to the dispensary and they cleaned out the toenail some more. He'd cut his shins as well and they bandaged his leg from his toe right up to his knee so he wouldn't get tropical ulcers – open wounds can play havoc, particularly with a white person. The next day he was quite delirious and I thought, 'Gee, I can't have him get sick here.'

So I immediately changed my plans, got in the car and drove him to Darwin, non-stop – I just filled up with petrol and kept going. He was in hospital for about four days because of this injury.

While I was there I met up with some other relations. With Jacob Roberts, who was my nephew, I ended up fishing around Darwin with another relation of ours, Lesley Joshua. We borrowed a dinghy and an outboard motor and I had enough money for some petrol so we could go hunting and fishing.

I had a great time with Jacob. He was a very knowledgeable person, too, though he wasn't that much older than me. He was brought up in Roper River, but was closely related to me; I was starting to find relations all the time like this. Jacob told me all sorts of things about ceremonial life and stories about the country. He eventually became a lay preacher and officiated at my mum's funeral many years later.

What was good, coming back to the Territory, was to find the relationships with the others. My mother said, 'You must learn from these other people.' The teaching I needed was not her role. She meant people like Musso, who I didn't meet on that first trip. Musso Harvey was my mother's brother, my full ceremonial uncle and a very powerful man in the traditions of Borroloola. And Old Tim, and people like Jack Isaac, Musso's brother. To discover all those relationships around me – all those uncles, aunties, brothers and sisters and so on – was very good.

For nine months in 1971 I travelled on an overseas scholarship, the Winston Churchill Fellowship, where I studied the histories and cultures of indigenous peoples in New Zealand, Hawaii, Alaska, the United States and Canada. I looked at multiracial programs in London, then travelled to Sweden to look at the indigenous Laplanders there – the Same people, as they call themselves. After that I travelled to India to see the Adavasi, the tribal people in the hills near Bombay (now Mumbai) to look at their self-help programs, too. One aspect of this Fellowship was to investigate how the cultures of indigenous peoples could be preserved in the context of the dominant society. Travelling overseas in my soccer days was very enlightening, but to look at indigenous peoples of other countries really put everything into perspective for me.

It was quite clear that we had to make many changes in Australia, and changes had to come sooner rather than later. Aborigines had to change as much as the whites, but the whites had to make concessions for us to move into society at large. We were the minority. Being less than one per cent of the Australian population at that time, I thought it would be a relatively sim-ple task, but we had to fight every inch of the way and I think the resistance we encountered was mainly about race rather than about rights we were demanding.

Governments, both State and Federal, didn't acknowledge our most basic rights – they still had a policy of assimilation. Before that, their policy had been to 'smooth the dying pillow'. They thought we were all going to die out, and that the aim, therefore, was to make our extinction as painless as possible. At various times we were classified as full-bloods, half-castes, quarter-castes, octoroons – all measures of blood and various shades of colour which determined how an individual was treated. Full-blood? Left to die. Half-caste like me? Taken. Quarter-caste or octoroon? Taken sooner.

When I came back to Australia I was full of ideas, and I think a lot are still pertinent today – ideas about the way we integrate people, the education system, how to acknowledge the old people within the traditional culture as the basis of the family. Family is important, it's the basis of human society, and yet we still try to push aside the old people, who have all the knowledge, customs and ceremonies.

We've had a lot of land granted in the Northern Territory since the Commonwealth Land Rights Act in 1976, and various Acts in other States, came into force. Land is very important to us and land rights issues are still pertinent today. Land has to be incorporated in any policy of integration of Aboriginal people into society at large.

I'm not into tokenism, nor am I wanting to make Aboriginals special in these areas. I think Aboriginality is very important to old and young people alike, but it should be taught by the old to the young. That doesn't mean to say we should be teaching all these things in institutions. For instance we can't teach our people sacred, secret dances in schools – that must be done out there in a proper cultural setting in the bush. The ceremonies must relate to the land. Those ceremonial lines that you belong to, those songs, either you have them or you don't – and already many Aboriginal people don't have them.

I don't think you can ever resurrect some of those lost songs and ceremonies, but what you can do is give those people an identity that will allow them to stand with their heads held high and not be seen as inferior. Many European immigrants, such as the Italians, have done this successfully – they've transplanted themselves here and become citizens of Australia but they still hold onto their family values and hand down their language and their traditions to their younger people. Of course, those may fade in time, but I don't think your heritage is ever completely forgotten.

What we've done in the past – and Aborigines are to blame in this as well as the whites – is get conned into accepting the dregs of white society, instead of the best white society has to offer.

While on that study tour I also made a point of going to Geneva to visit the United Nations Human Rights Commission. I'm sure I must have been the first Aboriginal person to go there and petition them for better rights for Aborigines: 'I want you to know you should be helping us achieve equality. Australia is a signatory to the Universal Declaration of Human Rights and we should have better access to your institutions to bring about greater changes so that we can have equality in our country.'

Saltwater Fella

Many delegations have gone there since. They're still going. I'm not sure how much impact they're having, but I think that early visit must have had some influence.

Chapter 8

Making

connections

Working with Charlie Perkins at the Department
of Aboriginal Affairs in Canberra in the 1970s

RETA MERRICK WAS AN ARABANA WOMAN. Her father was a Dieri man, her mother was Arabana. Reta's mother was Merna Merrick, whose maiden name was Merna Warren. Her father was Francis Dunbar Warren, who owned Finnis Springs Station and had about nine children.

I met Reta while I was doing university vacation work with the State Department of Aboriginal Affairs. A fellow called Jeff Pope, who was on the department's Advisory Board, said, 'Why don't you go and work on Davenport Aboriginal Reserve during the vacation and get a feel for the life up there?'

I said, 'Yeah, that would be great.'

When I first got up there, Pat Lennard, who was superintendent of Davenport Aboriginal Reserve, and Graham Smith, one of the staff there, said, 'Okay, drive the grader around the oval to level it out.'

That was supposed to be my job for the community, but I said, 'No, I'm not doing this.' So in the end I worked in the office and started meeting the people. I got to know quite a few and really liked them – people like old Malcolm McKenzie and Rachel Brady, who was a very strong fighter for her people. And I got to meet Reta and her family – and I started a relationship with her.

Reta spoke Arabana, and she was a strong individual, with a strong mind and a strong temper. She was a bit like me, particularly the temper. I got on extremely well with her family and I thought, 'She's involved in Aboriginal affairs. So, like minds, like activities, we'll probably get on.'

I found that we did get on pretty well, in lots of ways. She eventually came down to Adelaide, lived with other people, and then we lived together. She was a short, attractive girl, and she was very committed to Aboriginal issues. Her family had had a lot of bad experiences and she had personally had a lot of bad experiences. I think that when she had to go and work in Port Augusta at fifteen years of age she felt rejected by her family.

It must've been pretty tough for her being a black girl in Port Augusta then; black women were considered fair game by all the white blokes at that time. She had experienced a lot of problems with the Welfare Department, too – with herself and her family. Welfare officers, the police and priests had a tremendous amount of say over Aborigines in those days. Welfare officers especially had enormous power – they could take your kids, they could send you from one part of the State to the other, just get you a pass and put you on a train. Reta's family had a lot of problems with those people.

Although our relationship was often fun, and we had a lot of common interests, there were always clashes. She often said, 'I'm not good enough, coming from my background, to be in this situation.' I had bought a house in Adelaide, in Hawthorn, and not many Aborigines owned homes in those days. I didn't pay much for it. It was just one of those things – a bit of good fortune and a bit of hard work.

Even while I was finishing my degree we had a lot of fights and arguments, to the extent that it contributed to my missing some exams. I don't like trauma in the home. I'm generally a placid sort of fellow and I'd rather have a relationship where you break up if it's no good. I suppose I was learning a lot, too. The problems were not all hers; I had mine as well. The result was quite tumultuous.

I thought both of us being Aboriginal would be enough, but other issues kept coming to the surface. In those early times she was constantly fighting government departments about her family. She pretty much lived for her extended family, and we helped a lot of them.

Reta's problems seemed to manifest themselves in our relationship. Of course, I had a few of my own problems as well, having been taken away. I soon found, too, that you need a lot of stability when you are campaigning for issues: while you're fighting outside, you don't want to be coming back and fighting inside. However, I thought our relationship had developed to a stage where it was worth considering marrying her. I thought, 'Yes, I'll do it.' Later, while I was overseas, travelling on the Churchill Fellowship, I decided not to marry her. Then I came back and I said, 'No relationship has an absolutely dead straight run. You have your calm waters, you have your ups and downs. I can cope with that. Maybe marriage will settle both of us.'

We got married shortly after I returned from overseas in 1971. It's not a really good way to get married, but we did it and it lasted seven years.

There were no children. Reta couldn't have children. That added to her frustration, and to mine, but that wasn't the issue. There were more issues than that. The fact that she was an Aboriginal and I'd married her because she was an Aboriginal didn't solve them. I'm embarrassed to admit that. I regretted marrying her under those circumstances. When it became clear that it wasn't working out, I felt I'd failed. I also felt a lot of guilt about the prospect of walking away from the problems that she clearly had as an Aboriginal person. Her family, her extended family, had lots of difficulties. There were internal fights within their own groups and a number of deaths occurred within the family ranks for one reason or another. We were aware of these deaths but the actual circumstances were never fully investigated. A lot of things were just dismissed. If white people had died like that, there'd have been inquiries; if there was a violent death, someone should've been charged. These unresolved issues hung over our marriage.

In spite of everything, Reta got a job in the Commonwealth public service in Adelaide, then in Canberra, and she held her own. She was a highly intelligent individual. But even with all that, it came down to how much she let a lot of issues crowd in on her and get in the way of the things she wanted to achieve. It came down to getting on with life.

As a couple, we'd get into a pattern where we'd develop friendships, then something or other would happen and that friendship would close off. Reta was a very astute judge of character, but often in a negative or suspicious or jealous way. That extended to some of the friends I grew up with, like Charlie Perkins, and the boys that were close to Charlie, like Vince Copley and Gordon Briscoe. Those three in the main were fairly close to me at that time.

Reta thought Charlie never liked her and she was right. I just used to say, 'Well, you're not married to him!' We were tied up politically with Charlie Perkins and Gordon Briscoe, but with Reta's personality and her strength of character, she'd often clash with people. All those things added up. It's not that you marry your friends, but there are circles you knock around in and political paths that you pursue trying to overcome the problems Aborigines face, so in one sense you are married to that system.

After I broke off my engagement to Diana, I wasn't sure which way I was moving. The relationship was a good one, but I broke it off. I thought the problem stemmed from the fact that she was white, but when I married Reta because she was Aboriginal, I realised that you marry an individual – a person that you love, that you can be happy with at the end of the day and at the beginning of the day and throughout the day.

Where Reta was concerned alcohol was an element in our break-up too, but it wasn't the dominant factor. Sometimes when she drank her personality seemed to change, but the real problem was self-esteem. Her low self-esteem manifested itself in endless arguments where she'd insist that she wasn't good enough or that I thought I was too good. She was a fiery sort of a person and it all came out in the arguments we had.

I could see the break-up coming for a long, long time but I persevered. Coming from my background, with my religious upbringing and the way I felt about leaving, I persevered.

In the seventies the political focus started shifting more and more towards Canberra. Voluntary organisations such as FCAATSI were being undermined by the funding of other bodies from the Federal coffers, and their influence began to wane. I knew that change was inevitable, but I was disappointed that FCAATSI had to change because it was the one national organisation that was independent of government influence. That, I thought, was essential; Gordon Briscoe was very strong on that, too.

One thing Gordon did was put up a motion to change the name – everyone thought FCAATSI was a mouthful and the motion suggested changing it to National Aboriginal and Islander Movement – NAILM. Under the organisation's constitution a vote on a major motion such as this couldn't be held until the following year.

Gordon often punned, 'We're gonna nail 'em after this.' But what it did was nail FCAATSI. The following year the vote was taken, the name was changed and shortly afterwards the organisation fell apart.

Of course, there were problems with FCAATSI before that. A bit of animosity began to develop because the movement had its strength from the Northern Territory Aborigines like Charlie Perkins, Malcolm Cooper, myself and Gordon Briscoe – even though we had a great deal of support from key Aboriginal people across a number of States. The support we had was also backed by a lot of non-Aboriginal people who were involved in Aboriginal affairs, such as Faith Bandler, a Pacific Islander who was very active in Sydney; Barry Cohen, a Labor Party stalwart; plus a lot of other Labor people, the NSW Teachers' Federation and the wharfies. At the time the FCAATSI chairman was Joe McGinness, who was also from the Territory, which only added to the feeling of resentment among some Aboriginal people that the Territory people were having most of the say, most of the influence.

In the mid- to late sixties the Black Power movement was active in the United States, and Kath Walker's son Denis was among those who identified very strongly with its aims. Another was Bruce McGuinness, who'd come into the movement from the Aborigines Advancement League in Victoria. For my part, I thought the Los Angeles black was a far cry from the Australian black. My push all the time – along with people like Joe McGinness, Kath Walker, veteran campaigner Doug Nicholls, Gordon Briscoe, Winnie Branson and so on – was to forge an identity for the movement that was totally and uniquely Aboriginal.

There was another dilemma going for some young people brought up in the cities. Often those Aborigines with fairer skin had tried to identify as anything but Aboriginal. To avoid being picked up by the police, they'd say they were Maori or some other race, anything but Aboriginal. Of course, that didn't go down well with a lot of Aborigines either. If you're an Aborigine you should be proud of it. There was a lot of conflict on this and it still goes on today; that's always simmering under the surface in Aboriginal affairs.

Ironically, my Aboriginal identity is one of the things that have kept me very focused – you must know your culture, you must identify with your land area, with your family and so on – that's the backbone of many successful Aboriginal people. The others just come and go, and those who have endured have been those who follow those principles.

There are many tiers, many levels, that add to the complexity of Aboriginal affairs. That's understood by some and used to their advantage, both for good and for bad. Some people have hijacked the movement and said, 'Yes, we support Aboriginal unity but I need that money from the government more than others.' Those people look after themselves. They get a good package from the government to do things but they don't solve the real problems.

After the referendum in 1967, the Federal Government had set up a Council of Aboriginal Affairs. This consisted of Dr 'Nugget' Coombs as the chairman; Professor Stanner, an anthropologist;

and Barry Dexter, an ex-diplomat of pretty high standing who was also the chief executive of the Office of Aboriginal Affairs.

Then, in December 1972, the landscape of Aboriginal politics completely changed, as did many other areas of Australian life. When I saw the Labor Party's 'It's Time' campaign, with Gough Whitlam and key individuals in politics, the arts and business all up there on stage it really felt like the Federal Government was about to take responsibility for getting things done.

After the Whitlam Government was elected, aspects of what they did were quite revolutionary. Assimilation was replaced by a policy of self-determination, which I think was a good thing in itself. It allowed people in the outback areas both to be themselves and to integrate into society – to learn the culture from the elders, but also to go to school to learn about the white system and how to cope with the future in the modern economic system.

Another element of Whitlam's platform was that the Office be made into the Department of Aboriginal Affairs, with Barry Dexter at the helm. The idea was to establish a professional body that could administer Aboriginal affairs and have an Aboriginal advisory body supporting it. So a consultative body was established: called the National Aboriginal Consultative Committee (NACC), it was the forerunner to the Aboriginal and Torres Strait Islander Commission (ATSIC), which has been the national policy-making and service-delivery agency since 1990. The NACC was to advise the government on Aboriginal issues and policy priorities. It would have an executive of elected members from all over the country, with the Commonwealth Electoral Office conducting the election. Only Aboriginal people over the age of eighteen could vote – according to the Commonwealth definition of an Aborigine at that time: 'Someone of Aboriginal or Torres Strait Islander descent who identified as an Aboriginal or Torres Strait Islander and was recognised as such by the community in which he or she lived.' The agreed system of voting was first past the post, and it eventuated that the NACC had members drawn from thirty-six electorates.

In 1973 I took up a position in Canberra in the Department of Aboriginal Affairs Consultation and Liaison Branch, which was responsible for the development of the NACC. I was national coordinator for the establishment of the NACC and held the position of Assistant Director; Charlie Perkins was the Assistant Secretary; and Ted Egan was the Director. The Minister for Aboriginal Affairs at that time was Gordon Bryant and we worked closely with him. He had a great deal of compassion for Aborigines and wanted to do the best he could for them.

Our unit also had the responsibility of drafting an electoral roll of Aborigines in each State. We sent people to all parts of Australia to register Aborigines. As it was the first such election, I knew we were likely to miss some – and of course some people who identified as Aborigines but were not may have been stuck on that roll, too. There was no way to judge for that first election who was or was not an Aboriginal, other than the fact that those who were out registering were deemed to have knowledge of the communities in their region.

The consultative process that led to the establishment of the NACC was often quite colourful. One of the early meetings was held at the Australian National University, Canberra. We called together over eighty delegates from all over the country – special people who were leading the fight for Aboriginal rights, from the major cities as well as some smaller communities throughout Australia.

On the way there, at Adelaide airport, I met two tribal people from Yatala. We were all waiting for the flight to Canberra via Melbourne. At Essendon Airport, we transferred to a Viscount propjet plane, but immediately after take-off we struck really bad weather. I'm not the best of travellers but I just battened myself down with my seatbelt and held on.

It was the worst storm I have ever experienced in a plane. We were dropping hundreds of metres at a time, just dropping out of the sky, then just as suddenly we would lurch up again, as well as being shaken from side to side. The overhead luggage compartments were open and, during the turbulence, cushions and pillows and coats and things were thrown everywhere. There were two flight attendants; the one in the section where we were had to hold onto a child and this child screamed at every drop. This went on until we'd just about landed in Canberra.

When we got out, we were all really happy to put our feet on the ground. I looked at those two tribal fellows as we were heading out of the plane, and they had turned grey. We walked inside the terminal building and they asked me, 'When are we going home?'

I said, 'We'll be flying back in two days' time.'

They said, 'No, we're not flying anymore. We're catching the train!'

Anyway, the meeting was chaired by Joe McGinness, a gentle person who'd been involved in Aboriginal affairs for many years and who always spoke very slowly and deliberately.

Bruce McGuinness, who was fair in colour and not readily recognisable as Aboriginal, was also at this meeting. He was considered a radical in Aboriginal issues. He got up and was saying things like 'These whites are no good, they've given us a raw deal. What we want is . . .' and away he went with these ideas that would never be accepted, certainly not as a program that could be implemented by the government.

We all listened and while he was talking old Mrs Marge Tucker became quite visibly agitated. Marge was a very elderly lady from Victoria, a grand old lady who'd fought for the Aboriginal cause for many years; she must have been seventy or eighty at this time and she walked with the aid of a stick. When Bruce started talking about guns and getting the whites and we'll show 'em, Marge couldn't contain herself. She jumped up and started waving her walking stick and yelling out, which was quite uncharacteristic of her.

She said, 'Just a minute young man, just a minute.'

Bruce McGuinness was still talking in his rapid-fire way. Everyone yelled out, 'Give her a say. Let Marge Tucker speak.'

Marge was in full flight and she kept talking over the top of

Bruce McGuinness. Everyone started yelling, 'Microphone, microphone!'

Marge was so agitated she just kept talking. Then someone had the idea of taking one of the microphones off its stand in the aisle and passing it to her. She kept talking until finally she grabbed the microphone. Then she put it to her right ear and said, 'Now let me tell you, young man.'

Of course, everyone promptly burst out laughing and, when she realised what she'd done, Marge sat down and burst out laughing, too. She was a big lady and there she was, lying back in her seat laughing and that really broke the meeting up. Needless to say, Bruce McGuinness didn't get his way but old Marge Tucker definitely had her say.

One of the things we fought to obtain for the NACC was salaries for the elected delegates. The Minister for Aboriginal Affairs, Gordon Bryant, was a good person to deal with, but he was answerable to an Aboriginal Affairs Committee and this committee was dominated by two Queenslanders, Senator Jim Keefe and Manfred Cross.

We had advocated a Class 6 grading, which at that time was a class above the vocational officer level and carried a salary that was quite good for the time. Our proposal was knocked back by the Aboriginal Affairs Committee; the main person to argue against it was Manfred Cross, who thought a Class 6 salary was too much money for such a position. Furthermore, the Aboriginal Affairs Committee didn't want delegates representing

Aborigines on a paid basis. They thought the NACC should be more of an advisory committee.

In hindsight, with the way ATSIC has gone, I can understand his viewpoint. In recent years, it's been revealed that some people have been paid disproportionate amounts of money for the amount of work they have done. To some extent, Manfred Cross and the Aboriginal Affairs Committee foresaw these problems.

However, it was also a Labor Party Committee and in the early days I found Labor Party supporters were often the ones who found it hard to give Aborigines concessions, and this tempered my reaction to our setback. On the other hand, I always found Nugget Coombs to be a person with a great deal of vision in Aboriginal affairs. He was a powerful advocate of equal rights for Aborigines and an outstanding Australian of great intellect. He was utilised very well by people like Whitlam, but less effectively after Whitlam was sacked.

People like him – the great brains of Australia – should still be utilised. Heads of industry should be involved in Aboriginal affairs but they're not. We didn't involve those sorts of people much in the early days because we were trying to push self-determination, but we need such individuals behind us. I still think the approach we adopted at FCAATSI was a good one – bringing Aborigines into the mainstream of Australian society meant they would be less disadvantaged. However, the pace at which people like myself wanted to bring about changes was too fast for the public at large, including Aborigines.

While a lot of Aborigines were keen to move away from their poverty-stricken past and their political, social and cultural impotence, I found the changes that people like myself at the Canberra level pushed for began to move too quickly. We were isolating ourselves with concepts and programs that were too radical, and these exaggerated people's inbuilt resistance to change.

We had put into place mechanisms, particularly within the Commonwealth Government, to have Aborigines take up positions: the Department of Aboriginal Affairs was looking for staff, and State Departments of Aboriginal Affairs were looking for talented and qualified people to handle Aboriginal issues. Aboriginal organisations established as a result of the Whitlam era and the self-determination programs were beginning to employ Aboriginal people as well.

However, the structure of these organisations was often too lax. We allowed for some mistakes to be made while these organisations were finding their feet, but the tolerance level was greater than we'd imagined. People made some dreadful mistakes. People who were not the best were put in positions. For instance, people given managerial roles quite often employed their friends or their relations in the positions they managed. That's how some organisations either developed or floundered. The people that were good were promoted, but the people that did not come up to standard still remained in those organisations and developed their power bases.

As time went on and those organisations had access to greater funding, the problems were further accentuated. This has been to the detriment of Aboriginal organisations but it also hinders the momentum of Aboriginal affairs at the community level.

This is what we are reaping today as a result of the amount of funding that has gone into Aboriginal affairs through ATSIC. We didn't construct the organisations as well as we should have, and that's where we're paying for it now. Part of the solution is to require sound business planning for every Aboriginal community in the country. It might be painful but there should be audits (financial and structural) and accountability, as you'd expect with any organisation.

Of course, in the early days, from the time the Whitlam Government came into power and the Commonwealth Department of Aboriginal Affairs was established, people like myself had the vision of short-term programs that would enable people to move into mainstream jobs. I soon found out that this was not to be. Aboriginal people were only utilised by the various departments to liaise with Aborigines.

During this early period, Charlie Perkins was the only Aborigine in an Assistant Secretary position. He was able to sit in at the senior officers' meetings with the Head of the Department, Barry Dexter, and he was able to give an account of what his section of the department was doing. He also had a say in the policy approach of other sections of the department.

Within the department, Charlie Perkins was very strong on self-determination. I supported him and said, 'Yes, Aborigines should be heading that department.'

And not just there. I thought they should be in other areas within the Federal public service, and of course the State public service because Aborigines were reliant on many of their services. We pushed very hard to have Aborigines run Aboriginal Affairs and eventually Charlie Perkins became Secretary of the Department. Then the process was reversed, particularly at the senior levels of the department. At the lower levels more Aborigines were employed, but it seemed that people in senior positions met with a lot of resistance.

The NACC, once it was established, had to feel its way too because it was quite a revolutionary move to have representatives from all over the country. Most of these people were under-employed, virtually uneducated; many had grown up through the school of hard knocks. And here they were, thrust to the forefront of Aboriginal affairs, meeting in Canberra and being asked to give their views on how a Commonwealth Department should be run and helping to establish policy for Aborigines at a national level.

During this early period of the NACC we faced a steep learning curve if the delegates' views were to be presented in a form the government could implement. At the time, Charlie Perkins, as head of the Consultation and Liaison Branch in the department, was responsible for calling the meetings and so on. It seemed I was gradually being phased out of that role, even though I'd developed a great deal of trust with quite a number of these people. I found myself being isolated further and further, particularly as I found the role of the NACC was changing.

Charlie had a strong voice within the department, whereas the NACC had to convince the department that the philosophies or policies they were advocating should be adopted. Most weren't.

At the time housing was pretty well non-existent for Aborigines anywhere outside the cities. Even in the cities Aborigines had limited access to housing, particularly public housing. If you haven't got housing, you've got bad health; and if you're camping where there's no running water, it's just bad. The mortality rate with infants was high then, and it's still high now. Even today we have endemic diseases that shouldn't exist in modern Australia. Malnutrition is still very bad. Now we've also got AIDS, which could wipe out a whole generation of Aborigines, yet it's still not being tackled properly. Diabetes is bad, and trachoma was bad until the Fred Hollows Foundation launched the National Trachoma and Eye Health program in 1995, with the help and inspiration of Gordon Briscoe. He also wanted the Fred Hollows Foundation to establish a national diabetes program, but this wasn't done. It was apparently stymied in the Department of Aboriginal Affairs during Charlie Perkins' period as First Assistant Secretary, which is a real pity.

In 1974 I was elected Chair of the National Aboriginal Day Observance Committee (NADOC, later the National Aboriginal and Islander Day of Celebration, NAIDOC), a position I held for thirteen years. When I was elected it was much to the relief of the previous chair, Reverend Ron Denham, who had always felt uncomfortable in that role, being a white person.

NADOC played a significant role in the process of forging links with white Australian society. I thought NADOC was one occasion when we could present Aboriginality and Aboriginal institutions in a way Aborigines wanted.

In lots of communities you could have significant impact because of the size of the population, and the white community already had some links with Aborigines, particularly in country towns, like Port Augusta. Most country towns took up the issues enthusiastically, partly because the proportion of Aborigines is much greater in those areas than in the cities. We were often able to get into city councils, town councils, and organise things like raising the Aboriginal flag as part of the ceremonies to honour the day.

Around the same time I also took on the position of Chair of the Asia–Pacific zone of the 2nd World Black and African Festival of Art and Culture (FESTAC), which was originally planned for 1975, but rescheduled for November 1977.

When FESTAC came to my attention, I identified with it immediately. My first visits overseas had made me realise that the attitude in many countries to people of different colour, race and creed was much better than in Australia. When I found out that the African link was there I grasped it with both hands. I thought that I would be able to make a real contribution to my country, as an Aboriginal – but little did I realise how eventful this would turn out to be.

In 1975, I was returning from a FESTAC meeting in Nigeria with Kath Walker and a white fellow called Chris McGuigan.

We flew from Kano, in northern Nigeria, to Beirut, where we boarded a British Airways flight for Singapore via Dubai. When we landed at Dubai, it was early evening and I'd fallen asleep. Kath was asleep, too. We were next to each other in the second row, and Chris McGuigan was across the aisle. He woke me up and said, 'Do you want to come for a walk? We're in Dubai.'

I said, 'No, I'm tired. I'll keep on sleeping.'

I thought someone should go with him, so I gave Kath a nudge and asked her, 'Would you like to go for a walk with Chris?'

She was in a sleepy haze and said, 'No. You go.'

As I was walking off the plane with him, the hostess asked, 'Have you got your passport?'

I went back to the locker above where I was sitting and got my red Qantas folder with my papers in it. Then I went to join Chris, and we walked off the plane together. We'd just got down the gangplank and were heading towards the terminal when we saw these people in Arab dress running towards the plane; one of them bumped into me as he went past. The plane was about 100 metres away and, as they neared the plane, we heard shots being fired. A ground crewman was at the base of the stairs to the plane. He was shot. He fell to the ground and he didn't move. There was a flight attendant shot as well, although I don't think she died.

As the gunmen reached the top of the stairs, they started firing at people near the plane. Chris and I took off, running, for the terminal. Kath was still in the plane.

We waited and waited. We could see movement at the door

of the plane and, after two or three hours, they moved the stairs away and the plane took off with Kath in it. I thought, 'What's going to happen to her?' I was really worried for her safety.

Those of us who were left behind were eventually bundled into a bus and taken to Dubai proper. We were all kept together; we weren't allowed to go anywhere. I had nothing except my passport and papers. It must have been about twenty-four hours or so later when we were allowed to board another plane to go on to Singapore. I made a quick connection to Australia and when I got there the papers were full of the hijack.

In Adelaide, where I was fairly well known, the paper had a story about the hijack that made it sound like I'd been killed. There was a big front-page headline saying 'Two killed' – and my photo. You had to read the story to realise I was still alive.

Trapped on the plane, Kath ended up being flown all over the Middle East, as the hijackers tried to gain permission to land. Finally Libya allowed the plane to land. I saw TV coverage of it some time later, of the plane way out on the tarmac. When we next met up, Kath told me that she had woken up to the sensation of cold metal against her forehead. She opened her eyes and looked up and there was a gun in her face. Apparently a Swiss–German banker who had been in the row in front of us was shot dead during the altercation in Dubai. Kath said the plane had eventually run out of fuel, the airconditioning had stopped and they had even run out of water. She told me she wrote some poems while she was on that plane to pass the time.

In the course of the hijacking, the Arabs on the plane somehow found out that Kath was an Aboriginal person and that she was involved in the movement for equality for Aborigines. That may have been one of the things that allowed her to come out of it all unharmed. She was released and flown to London.

I guess I was pretty lucky not to get gunned down at the base of that plane. Joe McGinness always laughed about me running across to that terminal building. 'Yes, this fella here,' he'd say, patting me on the shoulder, 'is the only Aborigine in the desert in the Middle East to run 100 metres under ten seconds on his knees.'

When Nugget Coombs and Gough Whitlam met the organisers of FESTAC, they thought it was an excellent idea and encouraged Aboriginal involvement. I developed it from within the Department of Aboriginal Affairs although I'm sure it wasn't very well received within the department. Barry Dexter put up with it.

FESTAC turned out to be fertile ground for Aborigines to make a contribution to the international cultural field. It enabled us to put on traditional dancing, to present papers on political issues, to develop Aboriginal writing and poetry – all within the context of being black in Australia. We exhibited our art and a tribal collection was presented to the Nigerian Government. They would be worth a small fortune now, those huge Pintubi paintings. They're in Lagos, and one of these days I'd like them to be shown, along with new work, across Nigeria, possibly throughout Africa.

Nigeria was very quick to recognise that Aborigines were here, were disadvantaged and needed help. There were a lot of countries like that. Support can be shown in lots of ways and putting a cultural performance on in Africa, with representatives from many African nations there to see it, stood us in good stead.

At the same time, it showed us that there were a lot of disadvantaged people outside Australia, as well as in Australia.

Back in Australia, the Minister for Aboriginal Affairs, Gordon Bryant, was replaced by Jim Cavanagh. Cavanagh was a unionist and a plasterer by trade whom I'd met on previous occasions during my Amalgamated Engineers' Union days. I'd always found him totally unsympathetic to the Aboriginal cause.

I thought that was a bad call by Whitlam to have Cavanagh take over that role. Charlie Perkins agreed – he was at loggerheads with Cavanagh. In 1975, just before Whitlam was sacked, Cavanagh was moved to another portfolio. I was enraged when the Whitlam Government was dismissed, but I was also relieved that Cavanagh was gone.

After Whitlam's government was dismissed, Charlie Perkins and I went to see the caretaker Prime Minister, Malcolm Fraser, and the Shadow Minister for Aboriginal Affairs, Peter Rae. Rae had already been telexing Aboriginal organisations all around the country to get their ideas. He seemed like he was enthusiastic and wanted to get things done.

Malcolm Fraser, on the other hand, actually fell asleep during the meeting at which we were discussing whether Aboriginal Affairs would be better run as a statutory authority, by Aborigines. Before he drifted off, though, Fraser asked: 'What can a statutory authority do that a government department can't do?'

Looking back, he had a point. Having a statutory authority like ATSIC isn't such a good idea because whenever someone points out the failings in the handling of Aboriginal affairs it allows the government to point to a funded Aboriginal organisation and say, 'Don't blame us; it's not our responsibility.' It comes back to balancing self-determination with accountability – and the elected government, through the minister, taking responsibility. The government should ensure that the correct structures are in place and working.

My work with the Federal Government often took me to the Northern Territory and Darwin. It was there that I met up with my uncle, Musso Harvey, for the first time since I'd been taken away from Borroloola. The whites called him Musso, after the Italian dictator Benito Mussolini, because they considered my uncle an ignorant black.

I was introduced to Musso by a tribal sister, Ruth Kakaren. She was based in Darwin, working in Aboriginal Affairs with the Northern Territory Government, and we'd met at various Aboriginal meetings in Canberra and Darwin over the years. Ruth was very bright and we got on extremely well. I was very close to her until her untimely death. She went into hospital for an ordinary operation but suffered complications. She was a strong, young woman with her life in front of her, but she died. I've been very sceptical of the medical treatment given to Aborigines in the Northern Territory since then.

Musso was in Darwin for most of the time I was working for the government, and I kept going to his place because he and his family were very supportive of me, trying to bring me back into the fold, welcoming me back. I got a great deal from Musso. Of course, it was good going back to see my mother and reuniting with all my family, but it was the missing pieces I had to pick up that I was very concerned about.

In the cultural context, and in terms of tribal authority, I wanted to know where I fitted in. I knew Musso was an important person. People kept telling me that – people like Ruth and Musso's blood brother, Jack Isaac, who was also the NACC representative from the Borroloola area.

Jack was a very quiet person; he was married to a woman from Queensland who was not the correct skin for him. I think this got to him eventually. His self-esteem was eroded and he died, in my view, a premature death. Jack always kept very close to me when he came to Canberra and I to him, because we had that commonality of family links. He'd fill me in on the family side of it, and he always referred to his brother Musso as senior to him. Ruth and Jack used to say, emphatically, 'Musso's your proper uncle – your full uncle.' Not only was there a family link but also Musso had tribal authority behind him, being what we call an elder, what we call a malbu. You don't become a malbu just by growing old; you have to have the authority that goes with it, presence, leadership and knowledge.

Musso had that aura about him. He was quiet but strong. If you incurred his wrath, you'd know all about it. He was a typical Borroloola person – calm, except under extreme provocation, when his temper would really flare and his strength would fire. He'd assert his authority in lots of ways, not only by his physical presence but by the fact that he could throw a spear so accurately. He inspired genuine awe among the tribe and others. Yet the man was so placid in his everyday life that that's the only side of him I got to know really well. However, I knew the other side was there because a lot of people extolled his strength and prowess as a warrior.

Musso loved the sea; he loved the Gulf of Carpentaria. That was his life. And we're coastal people, saltwater people. Musso's land went right through to the Bing Bong area and it was all very significant ceremonially for him. It was natural for him to go out on the boats, the coastal vessels: he went as a deckhand and later became a mechanic, looking after the engines. He travelled the Gulf, sailing right around Cape York to Cairns. He also did a lot of droving, through to places like Longreach and all through the Queensland run, right back to the Territory. He knew that land backwards.

He eloped with a Yanyuwa woman called Roddy (who is an auntie to me in the Aboriginal way) at the same time that Willy eloped with my mother, not long after I was taken.

Saltwater Fella

The 1966 ruling on equal wages for Aboriginal workers in the pastoral industry in the Northern Territory had its effect on Borroloola people. At the same time, the improvement in road and other transport links also meant that Musso, like a lot of others, had to move away from the land and take on other sorts of work. Apparently Musso took a succession of jobs and ended up working in Darwin with the Welfare Department. He had a Housing Commission home in Rapid Creek, a suburb of Darwin, but he kept in constant contact with the people in Borroloola. If there were any significant ceremonies, he'd be back there like a shot.

Even though I knew he was important, I didn't realise just how important he was until I got talking to him. We hit it off immediately because he was a kind, gentle person and he was always willing to help. He knew about my background and he had spent time chasing me, trying to find me. He was close to my mother, and in a way I think he was relieved because I was a very close family member returning to the fold. He was always an unassuming, understated individual and, like me, he was a bit shy in coming forward. We had a quiet rapport to begin with, but this soon developed into a very close bond after two or three visits with him.

He began immediately with the family. He kept talking about the family, reinforcing the links with the people, with the oral history, who's who and how we're all related. I started to take over, questioning him. I became very inquisitive and he was very obliging. He found me a willing student; he was the master and he kept feeding me information. No doubt I asked things that I shouldn't have asked at first, but he still told me and just said, 'You've got to be careful how you treat certain types of information.'

My questions went right back to my time at Mulgoa. Every time people there talked about the old system, told me how I could dance, told me how good a hunter I was, I enjoyed that. I was hungry for knowledge at all times and every little bit that I received from different people kept building up my knowledge base.

When I went back to Borroloola and sat down with my people, I had a lot of information from others living outside Borroloola. I'd piece it all together and say, 'What about that? Yeah, that's where we come from over there. That's the story from that country there.' That's one of the strongest connections I had with Musso. I was able to put the pieces together. We were able to talk on matters as equals, in the sense that we belonged to the same group. I was never equal to him in the sense of his stature. I looked up to him; I still do and I always will.

He was such a proud man, in spite of all the hard times he had to go through. He endured the assimilation programs in the Territory, the dispersion of Aboriginal people and the hardships this caused – all the time having to hold ceremonies in secret away from prying eyes and ears, to keep them going. It was a lot more isolated up there then and they could do things much more easily without being noticed. But at times the police or a welfare officer would still step in to stop a ceremony or to do something else that said, 'You can't continue with the system.'

Saltwater Fella

I found the best way to learn from Musso was to go out hunting with him. Both of us loved hunting. He kept reinforcing names, family and belief systems, every time I talked to him. I'd say, 'Oh, what about so-and-so?'

Sometimes he'd get a little bit irate with me, and, with a questioning look on his face, would say: 'I've told you that before.' I should have remembered whatever it was, but he'd put it in a different context every time, to enable me to digest the information. I had to ask him things a few times. He understood that eventually. In a different setting, a different place, the piece that you were told had to fit somewhere – and sometimes it didn't fit at the time he told it, but the next time he told it it fitted because it had been reinforced in other areas.

I have a tendency to link strongly with the land, as I do with people. People and place are two very important cogs in my identity. Once I get out on the land, everything fits. You can point somewhere out to me and I can go back to that same spot, look at the setting and tell you where you'll come to next and whether there'll be a hill or a creek there.

Musso would tell me who was related to what ceremony and where they fitted in. He would always talk in the third person and not put himself forward. If you looked at the whole conversation, though, you'd see everything revolved around him; he had so much authority, yet he was so modest.

For a long, long time, the only man with more authority than Musso was Old Tim, who died at a very ripe old age – some say he was well over 100 years of age – in the mid-1980s. Old Tim and Musso were so powerful that together they controlled not only Borroloola but way beyond – right on through to Arnhem Land – and, in the opposite direction, across to Mornington Island. Ceremonies, particularly the Kunapipi ceremony, were crucial to looking after all that land. A lot of other people had significant roles to play, but right at the apex of the authority structure you'd find those two men.

Musso was instrumental in passing on the bulk of the information to me. The other significant person during those early times was Leo Finlay. Leo and Musso were tribal brothers, both were my tribal uncles. Leo was able to articulate the intricate aspects of the kinship system more precisely than Musso. Although Musso knew all the details inside out, he wasn't a good teacher of that. Between the two of them, I gained a great deal.

Leo, Musso's brother Jack and all the old Mara tribal people that belonged to our group, and all the other groups, became part of the jigsaw puzzle that I was able to fit together. The Mara group went right through to Roper River, where my relationship linked in with people like Phillip Roberts, and his brothers Jacob and Silas, as well as the other Roberts, like Stephen Roberts and his wife, Roslyn. That's where the tribal names for my children come through, as well as my tribal names, right through to that country.

Leo was a very strong link in that group. He married a lady from the Barkly Tableland who had links with Tennant Creek. Traditionally we had links with the Warramunga people, too.

And the Jingili people, who Willy O'Keefe has very strong ceremonial rights with. He's passed some of those songs on to me. He said, 'These are yours now, my son.'

Leo was linked in with that area through marriage. The artist Ginger Reilly belongs to our family group, as does Roy Hammer, who is now the ceremonial boss of Borroloola. That's where my family relationships lie with that group.

These days, there are still a few people who can teach me. There are a few people in their forties and upwards who have learned a lot, but not to the extent of people like Old Tim, Musso, Leo, Roy and the Reillys.

Musso and I shared a liking for being out in the bush. I enjoyed nothing more than being out with him. We would always end up on the coast, on the water. We'd camp in that country for several days. Every time I went up there we'd go out. Often it would be just myself, him and Willy. Other times a couple of younger men would come to help out, under instructions from the older people.

I was always treated as one of the tribe, a significant member of the tribe and a family member. I had the good fortune to be linked in those ways, so I was looked after very well. Sometimes they went out of their way to get me out with some of these people. I would say, 'I want to go hunting today.' Old Tim would instruct one or two people to come with me and take me to different places in the bush.

Old Tim had very little use of his legs by then but he had a powerful upper body. His ability to hear words and sounds and language was so acute that he could hear someone talking dozens of yards away; he'd catch every word of an ordinary conversation at normal level. When I'd try in the Yanyuwa way to pick up words that he was saying, he'd correct my pronunciation. He'd go over and over it and he'd get quite annoyed sometimes because my ear was not attuned to the fine sounds that he was uttering.

Then he'd say, 'Now you understand that one, we'll talk about this one now.'

He was very much a sea man, linked with the sea. He still made the old dugong ropes from the bark of the kurrajong tree. In Yanyuwa, he'd rattle off to the others what he needed to make the ropes, then at the end of the list he'd say to me, in perfect English, 'You get me number eight nail.' These roundheaded nails were sold in hardware stores around the country and I'd have to get some and send them back to him. He sharpened the nails by hand and tied them very firmly to the rope so they'd bite into the dugong.

His speech was very raspy, but quiet and soft. If he had to raise his voice, he would – and his authority was paramount.

His wife was a strong tribal woman who knew the system backwards. Every time I'd sit with Old Tim, his wife would be there, but after a little while she'd drift away and sit somewhere else. I was close to her, but my role was to be under Tim and to learn and master the male system. She was a powerful woman; she knew the women's side of things and she knew that whenever I came, the conversations would deal with the men's side.

The women always have control in their areas and you'd see those older women as the bosses of the women's side of the tribe. They'd have that authority and the old men like Old Tim and Musso would have theirs.

Musso was much younger than Tim, but he took control quite early. Although he became a leader early, Musso still had to wait many many years before he could assume Old Tim's mantle. Then he held it until his death, when Roy Hammer took over. I remember Musso even asked me, 'What do you think of Roy?' I volunteered my viewpoint. 'I think there wouldn't be any better person to take over the role of the authority than Roy, for the group up here.'

People like Roy would almost automatically pick themselves. Their role within the tribe, their intellect and strength and authority was built up over a considerable amount of time. They had to have knowledge of the ceremonies, knowledge of the land, and management of the people and the systems – the white system, as well as the Aboriginal. But it's the Aboriginal system that takes precedence in the sense of who should take over that authority.

Back in Canberra, Reta and I were continuing to have lots of disagreements, lots of arguments, lots of traumatic times. When I look back at it now, I was earning good money then and we had a good lifestyle and yet we still didn't get on. We tried to do lots of things together, tried to fix things up. We had an eight-week holiday in Europe and I thought this would help resolve things. It didn't. We'd have meals out with friends and in those days I didn't drink, but later I began to enjoy a glass of wine. Towards the latter part of our marriage, a lot of things would come out over a meal with friends. It just kept building up and up.

I eventually came to the conclusion that I shouldn't be with Reta. It was very painful. People were offering me advice when I thought some of their marriages were shaky anyway. I sought advice from only two, maybe three people whom I felt I could trust.

I don't think my decision came as a surprise to her. She'd often spoken of the rift between us. She'd threatened to go, and on a couple of occasions I'd even said, 'Well, why don't you go?'

That was said in the heat of an argument but this particular time I didn't want to wait for an argument. I didn't want anything to impede the decision-making process. It was on a weekend, around mid-morning. I thought that would be a good time to bring it up.

We both agreed that it would be better if we parted. That was the end of the relationship and we went our separate ways from then on.

Reta moved out. She stayed in Canberra for a while, then went back to the house in Adelaide and working there. I ended up giving her the Adelaide house, which was paid for, and I continued paying the mortgage in Canberra. It was a couple of years from that time until the divorce.

That was not a good period for me. I felt a lot of pain and I felt a failure. I worried about how some of my close friends would feel, how other people would feel – which are things you should never worry about in such a private matter. A marriage is essentially a relationship between two people, but I was worried about her family. Many members of her family had married and split, so I was keen on maintaining a good relationship there, including with the family, just for my own peace of mind. When it came down to it, the people who said to me, 'Why don't you go back and stay together?' were the ones who I thought didn't have good, strong relationships in their own marriages.

Reta's situation certainly epitomised the problems that rural Aborigines face. Improving the lot of people like her was one of the things that I was fighting for and that, too, had its effect on me. It was painful coming to terms with my inner self, with the end of my marriage; but it was also painful for me to acknowledge that in some way my fight to help Aboriginal people had failed on a very personal level.

I tossed it around in my mind for a long time. It was quite a tortuous and traumatic experience. I felt bad about it before it happened and then once we'd broken up, I struggled with my upbringing, which had instilled in me the belief that marriage was for life. It took a bit of coming to grips with, and inwardly I was quite troubled about it. But by that time, too, I'd met Ros.

Chapter 9

Ros

With Ros, in the early days
of our relationship

In 1977, Ros Langham joined the Department of Aboriginal Affairs as personal assistant to Charlie Perkins. As soon as I saw her, I was smitten. Actually, when I first saw Ros, one of my thoughts was, 'I'd like to have my children by her.' It's funny how you think ahead on things like that. I guess that's one of the things about being smitten.

She had a manner about her, a freshness, exuberance and sophistication that I liked. She had beautiful skin, even though she had a couple of pimples at that time. She was always embarrassed about those pimples. She'd hate me saying this but later, when I was able to speak to her in such a personal way, I commented on her lovely skin, its fine texture and so on. Even her walk was one of the things I liked about her. Ros was understated in her discussion of her work, in her presentation and demeanour. I thought she had a lot of depth and as it turned out I was right, on all aspects.

All those things rolled up in one and I felt so good about her, yet I nearly messed it up because of my traumatic break-up with Reta and its aftermath. I thought Reta was vulnerable in lots of ways because I knew her personality, her changeability and personality swings. I was concerned about that and I still felt a responsibility for her. I kept telling myself, 'Reta is gone, finished', but there was still this legacy in my mind, I suppose. I thought Ros had no part of that and should not be a part of it.

At first our relationship was one like I had when I was a kid. Those girls didn't even know that I liked them and no doubt it was the same with Ros.

It was a big step for me to ask her to lunch, especially the way I was feeling about her. Of course, I've had lunches with people, invited people to lunch for business and other purposes, but I found this much harder because I really wanted to get to know her better. We had lunch at an ordinary place, a very ordinary place not far from the office, near Woden Plaza in Canberra. The food wasn't anything special – it was an Asian place, but they served sandwiches there.

For me, the lunch was only significant in that it began the process of getting to know Ros better. We had a couple of staff lunches as well. On certain occasions we all got together at barbecues, and I enjoyed those too.

Ros was guarded with me – not least because she was soon to be married. I knew she was getting married, but I still liked her. She got married, came back to work and we continued to work together.

For some time I had been finding Aboriginal politics in Canberra quite frustrating. Initially it had been quite exciting: changes were being effected and things were moving in the right direction, but after seven years I was feeling like a tiny cog in a great machine. I realised that changes in Aboriginal Affairs couldn't come as quickly as I'd like. Tackling issues such as Aboriginal education, housing and health was always going to be a long-term proposition. Setting up an education system, for example, we had to accept that degrees take years, and we wanted an educational process that would cater for from pre-school onwards.

Another thing I didn't like was that rather than integrating Aboriginal people into the wider society, a system had evolved in which they were treated separately. That often proved disastrous. Housing societies, for instance, were set up to provide decent housing, but the council infrastructure didn't automatically follow. Electricity, good drainage, good roads, rubbish collection – all those things local government bodies usually provide – weren't forthcoming for Aboriginal communities because they weren't assured of getting the money from the Federal level.

And if you're going to do these things successfully, you have to incorporate some aspects of the Aboriginal culture into them. For instance, a baby delivered by a midwife, in the traditional way, was rubbed with a certain kind of ash for cleansing and disinfection purposes. The baby won't catch any bugs or anything like that if it is done right, but it's not easy to implement such practices in an urban context. Also, if people were out in the bush they'd be eating better tucker, moving from one camp to another, and there'd be fewer hygiene problems. Flour, sugar, tea, and especially soft drinks and takeaway food, are all taking their toll.

Eventually I decided to leave Canberra. I moved to Melbourne to take up the position of Director of the Commonwealth Department of Aboriginal Affairs office for Victoria and Tasmania. Ros, meanwhile, had realised after only a few months that her marriage wasn't working. Not long after, it ended.

I kept seeing her whenever I could. I still felt strongly about her. Then she took a holiday overseas with a friend.

I can't remember who originally told me, but I knew that on my father's side I had cousins like the O'Sheas and the Kirbys. Then I met Bernie Kilgariff, a Liberal senator who was from the Northern Territory and had Irish connections. I had some political differences with him at the time – I was fighting very hard for the Aboriginal cause, giving him a hard time. He was a little conservative on the Aboriginal affairs front but he was very tactful at all times and since then we've gotten on very well.

Bernie had quite a good working knowledge of the white Irish community in the central Australia area. I mentioned the O'Sheas and the Kirbys to him, that they were cousins on my father's side, and Bernie Kilgariff gave me some snippets of information about the O'Sheas. From that I made contact with a May Ulyatt, who was May O'Shea before she married, from Alice Springs. I phoned her and arranged to meet her in Alice Springs, where she was living on the Gap Road. She told me about my father, and showed me a photograph of my father and herself taken at Castlegregory, a little village forty-five kilometres from Tralee, in the south-west corner of Ireland.

I sat with May in her lounge room, and she told me that my father was a beautiful dancer and a good person to be with. 'We had a lot of good times together,' she recalled. She mentioned he'd come over to Australia in 1928 and, from the photograph, she named other members of the family for me. I could use the leads she gave me to try to make contact with my relations in Ireland.

Apparently, the author Xavier Herbert had met my father as well. Xavier was a good friend of Joe McGinness and when Xavier visited my home in Canberra we chatted for a while and he talked about my father. He had a good memory for people and places.

I said, 'Well, what was he like?'

It turned out that they'd only met briefly, and he could only give me a limited amount of information about him, but I was grateful even for this.

The opportunity to actually go to Castlegregory didn't arise until I travelled to England in 1980, after the break-up of my marriage to Reta. As Ros was travelling in Europe at the same time, I harboured romantic notions of meeting up with her, but they never came to anything. So I said, 'Right, now I'll see if I can make connections with my family in Ireland.'

With Tim Burridge, a friend from England, I took a car over on the ferry and drove across Ireland to the west coast, to Tralee. I had a name and address for a John Moriarty at Castlegregory, and had made arrangements to meet him and his family there. John Moriarty, who was an undertaker, wasn't a relation but he'd invited us to a meal while we looked around. He and his family had also chased around a bit on my behalf before we came, and it was through his family that I met an O'Shea, Pat O'Shea, who lived around the corner from them. Sean, John's thirteen-year-old son, took me around there to meet Pat.

He was a little fellow, ninety-two years of age, so I learned, standing on the front step of his house and looking at me with these bright eyes. For about twenty minutes, I stood outside the front of his house, explaining about my father, who he was, and when he came to Australia. However, when he realised he knew the person I was talking about, he let me in.

Inside, it was a modest little house. There was a candle burning in the front porch and he said, 'Your father was here for three days in 1928. We went fishing.'

He told me the number of trout they'd caught and how they had to throw them all back because they were too small. I can't remember how many it was now, but he told me the exact number – from fifty-two years before! Then he carried this little stool across the floor and stood on it to look in a cupboard just inside the front door. He pulled out this fishing rod. It was in three pieces, tied together, and the reel was a separate brass one.

He said, 'Your father left his fishing rod here.' He actually said, 'He left this here for you.' He apologised profusely because the line had rotted since then. Then he handed it over to me.

We sat there talking. Old Pat was a famous man in Ireland: he'd been a great Irish Gaelic footballer known as 'Aeroplane O'Shea' in his day. He'd won one of the big medals for the best player in Ireland. As I kept chatting with him, I asked him about my father's family, and discovered that Pat's sister was married to my father's brother.

But when I tried to ask him some more about that uncle of mine, he just clammed up. If you've ever seen a tawny frog-mouth suddenly catch sight of you, they strike this pose with their head – they just look up and freeze. That's exactly how I remember Old Pat O'Shea, looking up as if he didn't want to be seen, didn't want to be heard, didn't want to be there.

We sat there in silence for a while and then I tried to break the silence just by talking about something else. He slowly came around and started talking again, and we had a very good session, Pat and I.

I later found out that my uncle and his wife had had a girl living with them as a domestic. Apparently my uncle had an affair with her and that caused a lot of bad blood between him and Old Pat. I never did get any more information about that uncle. I knew he'd died but as to where he was buried or anything else about him, that died with Old Pat.

Later, back at John Moriarty's house, they gave Tim Burridge and me a nice meal. It was roast lamb, no gravy – a very Irish meal, with a huge amount of boiled potato on the plate. And a huge glass of whisky. A huge glass. I had only just started drinking the odd glass of wine at that time, but to keep the peace and show a little bit of respect for them I made out I was drinking the whisky. I just touched my lips with it. At the end of the meal the glass was still full, this huge glass of whisky. I had to say, 'I'm sorry. I can't drink this.'

They said, 'That's alright.' And they shared it among themselves. So I thought, 'Oh well, that's good. At least don't waste it, especially on a new chum like me.'

While I was at Pat O'Shea's place John had kindly made a number of phone calls around the place, including one back to Tralee, to another John Moriarty. John the undertaker said, 'I'll get him on the phone for you if you like and you can see if that's a person you'd want to talk to.'

It was a very funny conversation. I said, 'Hello, I'm John Moriarty. I believe your name is John Moriarty. You spoke to a man from Castlegregory who rang you not long ago. His name is John Moriarty, he's an undertaker, but I'm inquiring about my father who went to Australia many years ago and his name was also John Moriarty.'

The voice at the other end said, 'Yes, I had an uncle named John Moriarty that went to Australia. Would you like to come round?'

It was winter, and in Ireland the daylight goes early at that time of year. Tim and I got to his place just about dark and knocked on his door. We chatted on the doorstep for a moment and then we all went inside. John kept chatting and I kept chatting. Tim Burridge is usually a good talker himself, yet all this time that I was talking with John Moriarty the undertaker, Pat O'Shea and now this John, he hardly spoke at all. He was just intrigued by the whole conversation.

We had a look at a heap of photographs and, as it turned out, I recognised the Borroloola hotel in a photograph that John had. And in that photograph was my mother.

I said, 'Yeah, that's the Borroloola hotel.'

I don't know how I knew it. I couldn't really remember the hotel – I'd only seen the remains of it when I camped there in 1970 with Jim Pierson, the American fellow. You can still see the galvanised iron, the verandah and the posts, but some of that was barely standing when we camped just near it. I recognised that part of it.

John Moriarty then pointed to another figure in the photograph and said, 'That's my uncle.'

That's when I knew for certain that this John was my cousin. That marked the end of my long years of trying to make contact with my father's side. I felt I'd really found it that day, late that evening. I felt a huge sense of relief. It's one of those things you can't describe. Great relief, and I felt really good inside. That night I had the best sleep that I could remember.

My newly discovered cousin insisted we stay the night, and I woke up fresh and bright in the morning. I remember there were twin beds in the room: Tim was in one bed and I was in the other. My eyes just opened really clearly and it was light. I don't recall what time of the morning it was but my eyes opened instantly. Above my head was this little picture. I looked up and it was uncanny because I could see this brown face looking down at me. This child's face.

I sprang out of bed and looked at the picture properly and it was a painting of an Aboriginal baby, from the old Brownie Downing series of paintings that was popular in Australia many many years ago. It was an Aboriginal baby, just a face.

I asked my cousin John where it came from and he said, 'I don't know. I like it and it's been up in this house for years.'

We had breakfast and then John said, 'Well, my Uncle Eugene – your uncle too – lives at Blennerville. We'll go visit him.'

We went to Blennerville, where John showed me my grandparents' home and I spoke to Eugene. He'd moved from the family home because of a fire and some other reason, I'm not sure what, into this terrace. It was very dingy, built on foundations of big stone blocks; I remember it smelt of coal, and was cold and dusty.

A whole heap of papers, letters and cuttings and information kept from the family home had been bundled into this house. I was itching to ask my uncle if I could rummage through it all and try to find things about my father and the family in general.

One thing I did find out that day was that my other uncle,

Uncle Joe, had died just recently. Neither Eugene nor Joe had ever married. I was told by my cousin John, and later by his brothers, about Joe and Eugene being bossed around by my grandmother. They helped look after the old people and stayed with them until they died.

That day we drove around to the cemetery not far out of Blennerville to see my Irish grandparents' graves. I saw their headstones. They'd both died when they were in their nineties, in the 1950s.

It was Eugene who finally told me the circumstances of my father's death. Eugene told me my father had died in Brisbane, probably of an alcohol-related illness, in 1961. Around the same time, I'd played soccer for South Australia against Queensland in Brisbane; I had a great time on the field in that game and I can't help thinking that if my father had read a newspaper article about the game he might have seen my name and made the connection. We were actually in the same place at the same time. But we never met.

At Blennerville I found out that not only was my father's name John, but also his father's name was John, too. From what I can make out, even his father's name was John. We've continued the tradition with my son Tim, whose real name is John Timothy Moriarty. He's named John from the Moriarty side and Tim after Old Tim from the Borroloola side. Tim says his first son will be called John as well.

In Ireland I found that they didn't even blink, looking at me and seeing a brown Irishman, an Aboriginal one. They just chatted away as if it were a normal sort of thing. That's what really inspired me about the Irish and being over there. Once they know you're a family member, you're readily accepted, just as you would be with Aborigines.

John the undertaker was so positive and it was the same with John my cousin. He didn't bat an eyelid. He just chatted away, let us in, had us stay for the night. My cousin John was born in London because his father worked there, but John decided to move back to Ireland, to County Kerry, and he settled in Tralee, where he was in real estate. He was keen on keeping in touch with the family as well, so when I came along that inspired him to maintain contact.

As it turned out, my cousin John died not long after I met him. I've stayed in contact with his wife, Morna, though, who's since remarried. That first evening when we stayed, the whole family was there – John, Morna and their daughter Maeve, who was thirteen at the time, and Darragh, Maeve's younger brother. They all went to bed and John and I kept chatting late into the night.

About three months after John died, Pat O'Shea died, too. I was sent the clipping by the daughter of John the undertaker, another Maeve Moriarty. 'Aeroplane O'Shea has died': the story was in the *Kerryman* paper, which is published in County Kerry. The article related the story about Aeroplane O'Shea making contact with John Moriarty, giving the fishing rod back to me and saying that the fishing rod was now in the safe hands of the Moriarty clan in Australia.

Although it was sad that he died, I felt fortunate that I'd been able to meet with him and make that connection. It must be a trait of the Irish to hold onto things. I get criticised for holding onto things but I'm happy to be able to pass this thing on to Tim, my eldest son.

When Ros came back to Australia from her travels in Europe, she got a transfer with the Department of Aboriginal Affairs from Canberra to Sydney, and later to the Riverina. She frequently visited the region along the Murrumbidgee River, meeting with the Aboriginal communities there. I went to Sydney a few times to meet her, and she came down to Melbourne to meet me.

When I started courting Ros there was nothing in my mind except: 'My relationship with Reta is over. That's been a big chapter, but I've got to get on with my life. This is the lady that I want to be with and I want her to have my children.' In the early days, my continuing turmoil affected our relationship, but gradually we developed a pretty close relationship and eventually she moved to Melbourne. She ended up resigning from the department, and together we rented a unit at Glen Iris. Then we bought a house in Northcote, which we renovated.

I was happy from one day to the next day, then happy again the day after that. I felt good, extremely good. I kept discovering new aspects of Ros. She doesn't come straight out with, 'I can do this, I've done that.' You have to learn over time what she's done. It took me a long time to discover that she was a pianist. She had also been a singer of some stature in her youth; she'd won many singing competitions. She had been offered a place at the Melbourne Conservatorium of Music, but instead she had moved to Canberra to study linguistics and anthropology at the Australian National University.

I kept learning that she had tremendous depth, a huge capacity for knowledge, and a good memory for detail. She still comes out with things that take me by surprise. She's fairly deep, highly intelligent and has an extremely strong personality. She'd have to have that to stay with me – sometimes I'm not that easy to live with. Well, that's what I'm told anyway. I'm beginning to believe it a bit now, although I think I'm an easy person to get on with.

When she first moved to Melbourne, Ros took a job in an Australiana shop selling opal jewellery and other items. She came home at the end of the first day and said, 'I can't last in that job.' Then she burst out crying. She just hated it, working in that shop. The problem was that the person she had to work with wasn't very nice at all. I said, 'You don't have to work there.' The next job she got was with the Overseas Service Bureau, part of the overseas aid program, and she enjoyed that and made a couple of good friends through it – including Helen Sinclair, who is now godmother to our younger son, James.

When we found out that Ros was pregnant with our first child I had mixed feelings at first. I still had left-over guilt from my marriage break-up. But knowing Ros was going to have my baby I was also happy, extremely happy. I'd always wanted a child.

I'd always said to myself, 'I'll have a child when I'm twenty-eight.' I don't know why that magical age of twenty-eight. As it turned out, I was forty-three. We hadn't consciously planned it but we'd always spoken about having children. And I wanted children. Ros knew that, and it was a pleasant surprise the way it happened. I thought, 'What am I going to do? I'm not used to being a father, or a potential father.' We were still not married, although we had the house in Northcote.

When we first visited them in Tasmania, Ros's family was a little surprised to see that I was Aboriginal. However, I don't think there was anything there that said, 'You shouldn't be with her.' Ros's father, who has since passed away, and her mother, they'd come and stay with us. They've been up to Borroloola to visit my country and my family there, and I think they thoroughly enjoyed going up there.

Ros's mother used to come out with funny sayings that Ros still chuckles about – things like 'I've been working like a nigger today' – with no malice at all. It was just part of the way that generation spoke, their turns of phrase. Ros is the least racist person of anyone I know. Her closest friend is a Dutch–Sri Lankan woman, Rosita Henry. She doesn't see colour, she just sees people as people. She's very caring and understanding about the racial issue.

I was present at Tim's birth, on 20 June 1981. That was something that was hard for me too, in its way. I was brought up to have only the women's side involved in such things, but I have been present at the birth of all our children.

I was so happy when Tim came. It gave my life a totally new dimension.

Tim was Ros's parents' first grandson, and when Ros's mother comes and stays with us she just loves Tim, just loves him.

When Tim was still a baby, Ros and I got married in Melbourne at an Anglican church, St Thomas's, on 28 August 1982. I'm pretty realistic about how a lot of people feel in this world about me being married to a white woman, and a white woman being married to me. We just live our lives in our area and find we're pretty comfortable. You get comments here and there, but they are from people of no significance. Who are these people? They have no worth.

Racism still exists, of course, but not to the extent it used to. These days a lot of sporting stars and movie stars are black, which breaks down a lot of the prejudices of young people.

And success breeds success. We're seen as successful in our business and people see us as people now; certainly the people we work with in business. Most Aborigines are pretty accepting: those who have comments to make about whites often have more white blood than Aboriginal blood in them. You get it on both sides but it doesn't come out in a way that affects me anymore.

Mind you, Ros was a bit apprehensive when she first visited Borroloola with Tim, on our first trip there as husband and wife, in 1982. The people there knew of my first wife, as Reta and I had made a few trips up there. Ros had been up there before on government business with me and had met my mother, but we weren't romantically involved then; the relationship hadn't blossomed at that stage.

When I arrived with Ros and a baby, people's initial reaction was that I had two wives now. They said, 'You're a real Yanyuwa warrior.'

I said, 'No. I'm not allowed to do that.' But they wouldn't believe me for a while.

The purpose of our visit was to introduce Ros and Tim and to get his bush names. Once that was done, Ros had her Aboriginal names given then, as well. Ros always comments that she found she was accepted readily into my community. Colour was not an issue, in the same way that colour was not an issue when I went back to Ireland. It was good in that sense.

Ros found it refreshing that people immediately accepted her for who she was. They said, 'Oh yes, this is your bush name. This is how you relate to us.' My mother said, 'You call me Yuwani' – which means 'my husband's mother'. Ros calls my mother by the name for the specific relationship she has with her, according to our classificatory system. That's why people fit in so easily. Right away, people know who you are because of the way you address that person.

Ros was given her bush names, like Wunnajubbi, which relates to a specific land area she belongs to; the rights she has by the kinship system through her skin name, Nangalama; plus the ceremonies she inherits automatically, particularly through our kids and through my mother and me.

Ros

While we were in Borroloola I sat down with Old Tim and Musso, who was living in Borroloola at that time. I said, 'Oh, it's a long way down there, living down south. And we belong to this country.' Not that I had to tell them that – I just wanted to reinforce the fact that I'm a part of the system, I want to remain part of it and I want to ensure that the link is there in the future, for my children as well as myself.

I was born there, so they knew who I was and what roles I should play. The difficulty with Tim was not whether he should be named, but what name he should have. To determine this, Old Tim sat with him, holding him, for three days. I've got a photograph of him with my son, Tim, as a baby. It's a good photograph of the generations. Tim is fair as fair. And Old Tim is dark as dark.

Tim was still a baby then, about seventeen months old. He didn't walk until he got to Borroloola. He crawled and got into all sorts of mischief in Melbourne, but he didn't walk until he got to Borroloola. Then he took his first steps – just after he was given his name by Old Tim.

To decide my son's name, Old Tim sat with him, felt him, held onto him, put his hands on him and formed a sense of his personality. Aboriginal traditional healing is done by touch too, because you get all the feelings through touch. Old Tim had that knowledge. Not all people have it, but he could do it in an instant. Some people have acute senses that can pick up those things.

If you knew my son Tim, you'd realise how accurate Old Tim

was in giving the name Bundian, the cheeky brown snake. The Bundian, when he strikes, can strike in a very nervous way. He can be striking quite furiously, willy-nilly, at anything that moves. Tim's very astute and very incisive in going into issues, yet he can shift tracks quite abruptly – he's a real lateral thinker.

To show you the range that just one family can have, Tim's the grandson of the Rainbow Snake, whose dreaming starts near Normanton in Queensland's Gulf Country and goes right through to the Mataranka hot springs, near Katherine, in the Northern Territory. That's just one Rainbow Snake Dreaming area. It encompasses huge land areas. It also links with the stars, the sky, the galaxy and the universe. These are the things that are not so well known, the complexity of the Aboriginal culture, and how we relate to all this.

Giving the name is important not only because it assesses your personality and your intellect and influences how you will develop later in life, but also because it relates to the land area and the ceremonies that belong to that land. It's all intertwined, like bringing all those pieces together to make it fit.

There can be controversy about names given to different people. Jack Isaac, Musso's brother, once said to me, 'You have a name called Baiju.'

I said, 'No, my name Old Tim gave me is Kundareri.'

He said, 'No, you're Baiju.'

That name belongs to a certain bit of country just to one side of where Kundareri is, but it is interlinked. Kundareri is thrust up into the area that links with Tim, Musso and Jack. All that land area not only gives you your name but your ceremonies and what responsibilities and authority you have in that area. Sometimes a balance has to be made for a ceremonial area and a particular land area, because the strength of that group needs bolstering. All those factors can be taken into consideration when putting a person into an area and a ceremonial life.

Those ceremonies cut across not only your tribal area but other tribal areas as well. That's where the other dimension comes in, specifying the intellect and the authority you have outside your tribal area – in external relationships, in bringing those groups back in for those major ceremonies like Kunapipi, in going out to those areas. Kunapipi is a highly sacred revelatory ceremony that includes the second initiation; it also includes rituals relating to everyday life, and to death.

The naming of my other children was instantaneous. When James was born in 1983, he was given Djawarrawarral, the dugong. James is a lot more predictable than Tim; he is more placid but deep and on an even, straight path. He links the sea and the land. Some people have rights to the sea and stories that belong to the sea. James is one of those.

In fact, in the Aboriginal system you're not born anywhere, you're found there. You gain your spirit both from where the conception takes place and from where you were born, so there's a relationship which governs how you're linked with that land too – as well as your family lineage.

Until you have them, you don't realise the extent of the happiness and the feeling that you get from your own children.

They grow from a baby that's lovable, cuddly, a little life in your hands – and yet, from the day they're born, they shape you. They have a profound influence on how you treat them and others in the world, on you as an individual and on how you see the world. A child keeps building on you and imposing their feelings on you. Even as a tiny baby, they shape you.

Our third child, Julia, was born in 1988. I was extremely happy when she was born, although I didn't know what a daughter was going to bring. Everyone says, 'Oh, you've got to have a daughter.' And they're right – she's brought such joy into our lives. Julia's skin name is Nulyarima (the two boys are Balarinji) and her Aboriginal name is Maraelu, which is the mermaid. Julia is an amphibian – half person, half fish – yet her songs start in Alice Springs. Her full ceremony starts there and goes right up to the edge of Arnhem Land in the Roper River area. It has its roots in time immemorial.

Roslyn Roberts from Hodgson Downs is also Maraelu, but she's very much older. She's a sister to my mother and, because of her name, is a sister to my daughter as well. It's passed down through that generational link to ensure that you cover the land with your ceremonies and hold those ceremonies together and maintain that land area so you can pass it on to future generations.

It's multi-layered. You not only have to know your land area, you have to get the full explanation and the stories that belong to that land so that you can perpetuate that system. The elders say, 'The law never changes.' That's part of our traditional system and that is why we are named in those particular ceremonies, so we can uphold the law.

I'm not sure how many people know that system now – who should be what, at a particular time. It's breaking down. Not many people know it and I don't know how much longer it can be maintained in that way. Whites might say, 'Aborigines don't have a written culture. They're barbaric, they're pagan.' But when you look at it objectively, Aboriginal people are deeply spiritual, and they've survived for at least 40,000 years, and there's some evidence that their culture has thrived for 100,000 years. And even in the harshest environments, they had a standard of living that was quite good.

My children have an appreciation of who they are at this stage, but they haven't fully comprehended the extent of their involvement yet. Once they start linking with the right people and filling in the mosaic of that culture, they'll realise the role they should be playing.

When my children were given their names it made me feel real acceptance. I thought, 'I'm part of that system.' For the first time since I was taken away, it made me feel whole. You can never feel totally complete because you're learning all the time but it was a significant milestone in returning to my country.

Now people say, 'Oh yeah, that's your land. You know that. You have control over that.'

I feel an integral part of that system, knowing that I belong to that area and that there are people who call me brother, cousin, uncle. I can move to the future with confidence. I feel secure knowing that I belong to a group, knowing there's a security I can get anytime by going back there. For me there is always a fallback position – not that I look for one.

Home is home. I feel I can't be buried anywhere but up there. I tell my kids, 'You were born elsewhere, you have certain rights elsewhere, but your land area is up there. Your base, the Aboriginal culture, is up there and that's where you have your security.'

They feel quite secure about going back there. They always laugh and joke that our relations come down and touch them and feel them and talk in the Aboriginal way, how they're embraced in that way – both physically and emotionally. Yet the emotional security is there. My kids identify very strongly with our people up there, as much as they can at their age.

Equally, I tell them about their Irish connection and about my wife's side of the family. They have roots in a number of cultures – the Irish, the Aboriginal, the Tasmanian through Ros's side. Her mother's maiden name was Jones, so that's Welsh, and Ros's father was of English stock. I want them to be proud of their heritage on all sides.

Chapter 10

Business and pleasure

Ros and I with former rugby player Mark Ella, Mandawuy Yunupingu (of Yothu Yindi) and athlete Cathy Freeman at the opening of the Balarinji shop in Sydney

FOR YEARS, RIGHT FROM WHEN I BEGAN WORKING with the Department of Aboriginal Affairs in Canberra, I thought there was a market for Aboriginal art. I mentioned it to a few people I thought might have been interested in promoting the idea – a couple in New South Wales, a couple in the Northern Territory and a fella in Queensland. I tried to get them interested because as long as I was with the department, I didn't see it as my role – although I was pretty strong on maintaining Aboriginal culture, especially through my involvement with FESTAC and as chairman of NAIDOC.

In the eighties, Aboriginal identity was developing strongly and there was growing acceptance of it. I still think it's relevant in helping people who have been dispossessed, both in the cities and the rural areas where they've lost their languages and culture and they're pretty well in no man's land.

It was also becoming more feasible to make a living as an artist or designer. So I said to myself, 'Well, why don't I take it on as a commercial activity?'

No-one was very interested, but I was keen on it and Ros gave me a great deal of support. Tim was just a child but he was being brought up in the city and we thought he should have his identity within his Aboriginal culture as well as in mainstream society.

We started very simply. I drew up some turtle designs and Ros printed them on a little doona cover she'd made up for Tim. I didn't know how to silk-screen print. I still don't. I know the principles but it was Ros who actually did it. I had no experience with design either but I've caught so many turtles, I know where turtles come from, so I just drew those and Ros printed them.

That was the first design. Tim used that doona and then James ended up with it. He's still got it. It's a bit tattered now, almost threadbare, but he still treasures it.

We began designing in earnest: we called our company Jumbana, the Aboriginal name I was given when I was born; and our design label, Balarinji, our sons' skin name. The kitchen table was our first studio. What we tried to do was get our designs on products that were natural. We wanted to combine Aboriginal design with Australian wool, pure cotton and pure silk. We thought that wool, being synonymous with Australia, would be an ideal fabric to start with; we thought that would be saleable, marketable. And with that we wanted quality.

The first company we tried to get to print the designs was in Melbourne. It was disastrous. We quickly found out that quality can be really hard to achieve. The waste on that first run was just terrible. When we looked at those lengths of fabric we could see where the printing didn't quite meet. It hit sometimes and missed sometimes. We rescued as much as we could out of those fabric pieces and tried to make those into products.

The good fabric became part of a George Gross collection. We were disappointed that the tags we'd supplied didn't make it into the stores, but it was a beginning. It taught us how little we knew and that we had to learn quickly.

One of our next moves was to get a good licensee, so we didn't have to worry so much about printing the designs ourselves. The first licensee was Alan Freedman of Fresca in Melbourne. He produced our first scarves in Japan. We tried to make them here in Australia, in Melbourne, but the quality was lacking and the price was just too high.

The first lot of scarves from Japan were done with so much more care and quality, we really couldn't do it any other way. Fresca is still with us today.

We quickly outgrew the kitchen table and set up an office in our home – a big bench we had made specially, and an office desk. Ros headed out on the road with our designs and the baby. I was still working for the government, so we hired a part-time secretary. They went to Melbourne and Sydney to sell products and develop the licensing business. Ros would walk into places where she thought there might be buyers and say, 'Can I show you some fabrics and products with Aboriginal designs?'

They'd just dismiss her. 'No, we don't like the browns and blacks. We don't like the earth colours, the Aboriginal designs.' Some wouldn't even look at them. 'There's the door.'

Ros had to talk her way around that. She was persistent and eventually she broke down some of the resistance. We really started by jumping in at the deep end. I'd come home and we'd work there at the business until one and two o'clock in the morning at times. We had to learn the business principles very quickly – day-to-day things like trying to get sales, putting together all the designs and getting them printed.

Ros was a tower of strength in all sorts of areas. Finance wasn't her strongest area but she picked that up very quickly. It was a steep learning curve for both of us, but she had to bear the brunt of it in those early days. You can't take that job away from her now, although as we began to expand we had people like our accountant Richard Wishart and staff members who worked alongside Ros.

I wasn't surprised by Ros's abilities at that stage. I had always had an admiration for her capacity. I noticed that really early in our relationship. She had a lot of ambitions, too, to do things. She wanted to be a writer, and she still wants to write. She wanted to pursue her music. That energy, all that creativity, all that desire, had to burst out somewhere. Being home looking after a child wouldn't have fulfilled all of her aspirations. We thought the business would be one way of doing that. We didn't realise what it could lead to, but obviously it took a great hold on most of her time and energy. The way the business is going today shows the amount she's put into it.

Back then, we soon realised that if I went out trying to get sales I wouldn't get in the door because I was Aboriginal. For me, keeping a low profile for those sales meetings was quite hurtful. I'd put up with that during most of my life really – being served last in shops, being treated as a second-class citizen. It still happens, but not so much.

Nowadays Aboriginal art is big business. Big money is being made, though not necessarily by Aborigines themselves. So it's a lot different today, but there's still a bit of a way to go before people really understand Aborigines as artists. We're the oldest surviving civilisation and we've looked after the country, kept it pristine for countless centuries. Our traditional culture has allowed us to relate to the universe around us in a way that is the basis of what humanity is all about. There's a lot of knowledge there, centuries of knowledge of the world and the formation of the landscape, the philosophy behind it. Art is one of the things that flows from that.

Despite the setbacks, it wasn't long before the business had developed to the stage where it needed to move on to the next level. Also at that time my involvement in Aboriginal Affairs was getting to a stage where government and I had outlived each other.

Not long after Ros and I were married, I was offered the job of Director of the Department of Aboriginal Affairs in South Australia. I went to Adelaide, and Ros and Tim came over later. After about two years, I was offered the directorship of the State Office of Aboriginal Affairs. By then, I was happy to make the shift from Commonwealth to State. I wanted to go into business for myself sometime, but first I wanted to make some changes on the State level that I thought were necessary and overdue. In positions like mine, I felt that personnel changes should be made on a regular basis anyway, at ministerial as well as administrative levels.

Before long, I was having problems with my minister, Greg Crafter. I thought he was weak: he didn't have much vision for Aborigines, other than keeping everything quiet and looking after himself – which most politicians do anyway.

I thought, and it was my mistake, that he had some convictions about Aboriginal issues and that he was going to implement changes, based on advice from myself and other Aborigines.

My push for Aborigines was quite clear – to get them working in good jobs in business and industry, rather than just in Federal and State government. Crafter gave me a vague undertaking that he'd do whatever was in his power to do. As it turned out, he just wanted to keep the situation as quiet as possible so he could get re-elected.

The Premier of South Australia was John Bannon at that time, and Bruce Guerin was one of his advisers. I eventually went to Guerin and said, 'I don't think Aboriginal Affairs is going in the right direction. I'd like to have a meeting with the Premier.'

He said, 'Well, if you don't like it, why don't you get out?'

I replied, '*I* shouldn't be out of Aboriginal affairs. You fellas should be out of it!'

Needless to say, my minister didn't like that, and I didn't ever get to meet the Premier. Not long after that, there were many changes in the State Government. Bannon lost office and Crafter lost his seat at the next election, but by then I'd already moved into the business full-time.

I was glad in one sense that I'd left the department. South Australia is a small State, a poor State, but I still thought what it was putting into Aboriginal Affairs as a proportion of its over-all budget was not what it should have been. I didn't expect miracles, but I thought we should reorganise some programs to make them more efficient and to give Aborigines more control and responsibility – in education, in housing and land issues. These things didn't need lots of money thrown at them, just different attitudes and the ability to act more progressively. All they needed was renewed vigour, creativity and commitment from the government.

Instead, Crafter kept people like Garney Wilson as President of the South Australian Lands Trust. I thought Wilson was pretty weak in lots of areas. He looked after one little area, his own people down in the Point McLeay area and Camp Coorong. I got extra land for the Camp Coorong people and he welcomed that, but when I was pushing land issues for people in other parts of the State, particularly the north and west, I got no support from either the Lands Trust or Crafter.

There were some landmark issues during my time there, too. The Maralinga lands were handed over in 1984, but I also wanted us to push for proper compensation from the British Government to pay for the clean-up after the nuclear testing.

Instead the Federal and State governments instructed Andrew Collett from Johnson Withers and Partners to deal with Archie Barton, who was an Aboriginal involved with the Maralinga Tjarutja group. And they effectively cocooned Archie.

I tried to get involved but Archie didn't want me there. I kept up the pressure for a lot of things to be done for the Maralinga people. I thought the deal Archie and Collett did with the British Government was totally inadequate. They were too soft and too compliant. It seemed like no-one was prepared to create a fuss or upset anyone.

That's where I got off-side with a lot of government people in those days. I believe Crafter wanted me out because of the issues I was pushing. I didn't like the wheeling and dealing behind the scenes that diluted the rights of Aborigines at every turn. The Maralinga people, for example, could have done much better. Everything was still out of our hands.

I think there should be more bodies like the Lands Trust set up by the New South Wales Government. It receives millions of dollars of funding: some is used immediately in the communities, but the bulk is put into trust and they use the interest to fund long-term projects. Those sorts of schemes have far-reaching consequences; they develop their own momentum. Forget the culture, forget the politics, it's essentially the dollars that can have that sort of impact.

However, those dollars have to be channelled by principled and astute administrators. I despair of some advisers, but that's where the vision must come – with those leaders, Aboriginal people and their advisers. In 1988, when I left the government, that was just not happening in South Australia.

Our business, on the other hand, was going from strength to strength. We'd begun with savings of only 12,000 dollars and our beginnings had been quite difficult but we had confidence in our business principles, as well as the vision of successful Aboriginal design to sustain us.

From the start, we aimed to show things overseas as well as in Australia. One of my mistakes was when we bought some Aboriginal art and artefacts from Katherine in the Northern Territory and had them sent over to Holland, where we displayed them with some of our products. We found the Dutch very frugal – we really learned what 'going Dutch' meant.

Then we were asked to show our designs in France, which we agreed to do. Austrade (the government's trade commission for Australian exporters) asked us to send products to them in Paris. We sent everything through normal post and the customs people seized it and demanded we pay duty on it. To get that product released, we would have had to pay more than it was worth. It's still there, as far as we know. That was a financial disaster, but when we eventually showed some of our products in France, we generated a great deal of interest.

We quickly developed better strategies, and learned to adapt pretty quickly. At times I did consultancies in order to survive. We chased up people we thought might help to promote our products. We planned to launch our first collection through the

Wool Corporation. We thought, 'That's a good start. And we could get Bob Hawke to launch it. Who better than the Prime Minister, who is sympathetic to Aboriginal issues?' Hawke declined but the Wool Corporation was very supportive, and we presented our designs on pure superfine Australian wool.

Our design style has changed over time, although I thought the designs for those early products were very classical, very timeless. Who knows? One of these days, I may even resurrect those original designs.

We found it very hard to get established in Australia – Aboriginal-design-based products were still not seen as marketable. What Ros did, though, when she went to visit places, was that once she was in there she began a dialogue – and that kept a few doors open.

But what really created interest in the Australian market for us was our Budget Rentacar uniform design in 1986. Those designs were timeless, too; they lasted many years. There was a winter uniform as well as a summer one, which was worn year round in the tropical parts of Australia. At that time that was our most successful design, our most visible at least. It did us a lot of good and, personally, it made me feel fantastic to know that Budget Rentacar, a national company (headed up by Bob Ansett at that time), overtly promoted Aboriginal designs.

It was a real breakthrough for us and, in my view, it was also a breakthrough for corporate life in general in Australia. It signalled greater acceptance of Aboriginal design and culture. That's one of the satisfying things that continue to happen with our design. While we push the commercial aspect, we also push the underlying idea that Aboriginal design is unique and build an appreciation of the meaning and culture behind it. I think that's great for Australia.

When the Budget management chose our designs I think there was a desire for things that are Australian, although 'Australian' at that time meant something Australian-owned. What we were pushing for was a little more than being Australian-owned, we were pushing 'Australia' as being the spirituality behind the design that makes it totally different from other cultures. That's something for all Australians and it psychologically links in to the ancient fabric of this country.

Gradually, people are beginning to appreciate that there is a unique depth of spirituality here. Not many people can truly understand the spirituality of Aboriginal culture, how it relates through design to people and to the formation of the land. Lack of knowledge is probably part of the mystique of Aboriginality, but I like to think that people are coming to understand it little by little through our art. Ros and I have been trying to impress on people (in my case for nearly forty years) that this is something all Australians – white and black – can relate to, so they can understand this country and feel more a part of it than they do if they think of themselves just as transplanted Europeans.

Whenever we thought we were down on our luck, we'd get a contract like Budget and it spurred us on. We kept going and gradually built on small successes. Working together isn't that easy at times, though. When the pressure's on, with deadlines to meet, the job continues to six or seven o'clock at night. Often it continues at home late into the night. It can be difficult to manage, especially with the kids growing up and needing time and attention from both parents. It's hard to imagine what it's like for a single-parent family, the kids and people in that situation. It can't be easy.

At all times we've endeavoured to stay together as a family. We talk a lot (we have our family meetings); we get the kids' viewpoints on how they see our family relationships continuing and improving – and particularly on their school lives and their social lives.

We've set definite rules. We have people in to help around the house so we have more free time together. We have a pact that we'll spend at least one day of the weekend together as a family. It's difficult when the kids have sport and other activities they pursue at the weekend, but we try.

We like to go camping together because that way you get away from television. And I like the kids to know a little bit more about nature and the countryside. I don't think living in the city brings many benefits for kids – they don't get the feel of what this country is all about. We try to get away on family outings. We travel together often – overseas, and back to Borroloola. We go camping just to stay together. People say, 'You can go and live in a hotel and do the same thing.' But it's not the same. I like to live with a fire. I think fire is one of the most civilising instruments in any culture. Smoke is important. The smell of smoke – looking, touching, feeling. I still like to go out to the countryside, smell the grass, the trees, the different sorts of plants, the animals and birds and things. It's important for kids, too.

For a while we had a shack at Corny Point, on the Yorke Peninsula in South Australia, and we went over there frequently. The kids loved that. It was on the coast, it was quite rugged and we made quite a few friends there. People like Dave and Bev Wyatt, who just happened to drive past one time when we were at our shack, introduced themselves and we became firm friends. Another person down there was Len Williams, who was a cray fisherman. We got to like Len and his wife very much. Len would drive past our place and stand on the cliff and look across to the west, analysing the weather and deciding whether he would go out in his boat to pick up the craypots. On occasion, we'd order a crayfish from him: 'Len, we're going to have dinner, a few friends; we'll be having so many for the meal.' He'd pick out some crayfish for us, cook them that morning, stand them on their noses to drain for the day and chill them. By the time we picked them up for the meal they'd be perfectly sweet and juicy, ready for the table that night. Those sorts of experiences the kids loved. I used to dive for abalone on the rocks and we'd cook some of those, or fish off the rocks and catch fish to eat.

That part of the world is magnificent, but then so is most of the Australian coast – you can make a nice haven in a lot of places.

Eventually we were able to find a new place that gave us just a little bit more isolation so we could get that true feeling of the bush. The coastal water system of the Coorong, south-east of Adelaide, is one of those few places in the world where you don't have your mind cluttered with all the superfluous issues of city living. You catch fish. You walk on the beach. You see the birds and animals. The bird life, especially the variety of waterbirds, is among this country's best.

I had been going to the Coorong since the fifties, visiting Champ and his wife Elva at their galvanised iron shack down there. In the early 1990s Ros and I bought a parcel of land right on Rob's Point, which was also called Wurrukurrum. It was part of an Aboriginal reserve that had been sold to an Aborigine called Robert Day. Robert had had the land for a couple of years or so when he decided he wanted to live in the town but he still wanted to keep the land in Aboriginal hands.

I knew Robert from the early days because Champ used to visit the Days at a couple of camps just outside of Meningie – One Mile and Two Mile, I think they were called. The camps on the fringes were just corrugated-iron sheeting with hessian bag walls in amongst the mallee scrub. You'd see Robert and his sister, Sarah, doing their homework by candlelight at these places.

Like a lot of Aborigines in the area at that time, Robert experienced exclusion and discrimination in town – all the worst aspects of segregation. When times changed, he wanted to live in the town proper and he wanted to live in his own house; he offered us the land to help him afford his own home in Meningie.

It was fortunate for us that the block was on a magnificent headland with a commanding view of the Coorong in both directions. I'd often talked to Ros about the Coorong and when we travelled down to look at the block she fell in love with the place on her first visit, which really pleased me. It was serene and peaceful yet fierce storms sometimes lashed the area. You could experience all the moods of nature there – its beauty and its anger. Ros helped to plan the house we built there, and she just loved it. We all did.

We did a great deal of living in that house, which was designed by Phil Burton, an Adelaide architect. We wanted a place that blended into the area, something that would overlook the water and the sandy coastline; something that could be open to the elements at times, yet where you could feel comfortable in front of the fire when storms swept through.

The place was great for families, and the kids were never bored – what with the canoes and the catamaran we had there, and the walks we did. We shared our special place with our friends, and we could have three or four families staying there at one time. The kitchen was designed so you could have people in it while you were cooking up a meal. We'd cook cockles we'd taken from the beach, we'd feast on mullet or mulloway we'd caught in the Coorong.

Then, around sunset we'd stroll outside and and marvel at the unspoilt scenery. Our house barely made a dent in such a wild environment – we just built into it. We could sit on top of the limestone headland there, overlook the glassy water with its reflection of a bright red sunset, and watch these huge flocks of waterbirds – from pelicans to swans and all varieties of ducks – fly up and down the Coorong. We didn't have to move. They'd fly right past us. We'd also see emus across the other side of the water, and kangaroos lived on our property.

The value of that kind of place you just can't measure. Tim, our eldest, was always saying, 'I'd like to go to the Coorong.' Even today, when we no longer have our place at the Coorong, having moved our business to Sydney in 1997, he misses it. He's a very creative spirit and he felt good there. James loved the physicality of the place – he'd hop in a canoe and make the voyage across to the other side of the lagoon or just paddle and play around in the shallows. Julia loved the water, too.

At the weekend, we could get down there in just over two hours, and we'd be set up all comfortable on a Friday evening. We'd have two peaceful nights there and recharge our batteries. Everyone appreciated that in their own way.

My family environment now is very different from the childhood I experienced. Like a lot of modern kids, when I tell my children about the circumstances I grew up in, they say, 'Yeah, that was back in the eighteenth century. You're in the twenty-first century now, Dad.' They might have a go at me every now and again, but they do appreciate the fact that I exposed them to places like the Coorong.

We camped on our block of land before the house was built and they liked that, too. We also camp when we go back to Borroloola, where the bush offers a different experience altogether. In that area the people hunt on a regular basis – for turtle, dugong, kangaroos and bush turkeys, and they fish and catch long-necked turtles in the billabongs. We get very close to nature up there, hunting and camping with our mob, sleeping out wherever we go. Sometimes we camp on the creeks and see crocodiles down in the water, not far away from us.

One time we camped at a place where my mother said my auntie had been buried alive in the sand by a policeman for refusing to carry a bag of salt – the bags of salt were as big and heavy as a bag full of wheat. We set up camp right on the water's edge, where the water is fresh; we'd camped there many times before. The water flows over the rocks into this huge rockpool, then it keeps flowing downstream to join a tidal saltwater tributary. It's a beautiful spot. We swam in the rockpool and you could see the fish in the water. You could catch them as well, and you could catch turtles, freshwater turtles – they're some of the best tucker you can get, succulent and mild in flavour.

This particular night we'd pitched tents because there were a few families there. We were about to go to bed and I was just shining the torch around on a bit of a headland when I saw this pink eye looking over the top of the rock. And it was huge. That eye was huge.

I said, 'We can't camp here tonight.'

We all had to shift. We camped high up on the bank then, way up on top. I knew that crocodile was a saltwater one. There were lots of freshwater ones there and we generally don't worry about them, but this one was a saltwater one and he was one of the very big ones, four or five metres easy. I took my family up onto the bank and we camped up there, out of harm's reach.

Chapter 11

Soaring

Graham Monro/Qantas

Ros, Jeanne-Claude and James Strong,
and myself, at the launch of the
Wunala Dreaming plane in September 1994

THE QANTAS PLANE DESIGN WAS ONE OF THOSE THINGS Ros thought of early one morning. It must have been about two o'clock when she woke me up and said: 'What do you think about painting a Qantas plane? It would be perfect for us.'

'Yes, yes,' I said, 'I know it would, but go back to sleep. It'll never happen.'

And yet we kept thinking about it – and the more we thought about it, the more perfect it seemed. Even down to the fact that the Qantas logo is a kangaroo and I belong to the Kangaroo Dreaming. At the time, 1993, Qantas hadn't listed on the stock exchange and I said, 'We can put our idea to them, but Qantas is a very conservative public service organisation. It'll never happen. It's ideal, but it won't work.'

Ros kept mulling it over. We were travelling a lot; I was doing consultancies, mainly on Aboriginal issues. I had participated in the Melbourne Olympic bid, we were licensing designs to companies like Nittobo in Japan, we'd done a launch in Paris with Sisel Sport, we'd licensed Ozart in Sydney. Things were humming along. By this time we had a team of designers, Aboriginal and non-Aboriginal, working for us.

As we became more experienced at working with consultancies and getting our ideas across, we realised that with Qantas we would have to get to first base right at the beginning. We couldn't start at the bottom of the company and say, 'Look, we have a great concept here.' It would take forever to get a decision.

The golden opportunity arose when Qantas hosted a promotional weekend at the Hyatt Hotel in Adelaide. James Strong, the chief executive of Qantas, and his wife, Jeanne-Claude, came over for that – and, being frequent flyers with Qantas, Ros and I were invited. We thought this just might be our chance to talk to James Strong. The problem, we thought, would be getting to meet him. However, one morning we found ourselves sharing the lift down to breakfast with James and Jeanne-Claude Strong.

Amazed at our luck, we didn't hesitate to raise the concept with him in the lift. And it just so happened that we had the design upstairs in our room. While I kept Jeanne-Claude and James talking, Ros went and got the 2-D mock-up of a Qantas plane, painted the way we thought it should be.

Now James Strong is very cool; he's a person who doesn't reveal his emotions, especially with people he's only just met. Well, when he saw the plane it really hit him. You could see it in his face. I've met with him many times since, but I haven't seen that look again. The design was so strong, that colour-saturated look with the paints. It was magnificent – well, *we* thought it was, anyway.

He said, 'Let's have a look at it. What you need to do is show it to Hans Hulsbosch.' Hans was the original designer of the Qantas white kangaroo logo. We went to his office in Sydney – we flew over especially to meet him – and when he saw the artwork for the plane it knocked him backwards, too. He had to step back a couple of paces because he hadn't known what to expect. He actually looked quite unsteady on his feet.

Quickly, I said, 'Would you like to sit down?'

He sat down, and I pulled up a chair in his office. Then he said, 'I like it, I like it!'

I think that was really the turning point. 'We didn't touch the tail,' I volunteered, wary of encroaching on the Qantas corporate image. Hans warmed to it quite quickly – and from then on, there was no holding back. James Strong summed up: 'This will make a really major impact.' It would've been all too easy for him to say, 'No, it doesn't fit in with our image' or 'It's too great a risk' – but he didn't.

Not long after, Qantas's competitor in Australia, Ansett, was licensed to fly internationally and their inaugural flight was to coincide with the opening of the new Kansai Airport at Osaka in Japan. Qantas was flying regularly to Tokyo's Narita Airport, but for their first flight into this new airport, they wanted to do something special to counter Ansett and make a real statement about flying into Osaka. Knowing the Japanese affection for

Soaring

Australian objects and Aboriginal design, Qantas – in particular Strong's deputy manager, Geoff Dixon, and marketing executive Garry Saunders – took a very bold step and agreed to have a plane painted with our designs.

We transposed our 2-D design onto a scale model of a 747 aircraft and then the model was computer-imaged. With the design computerised and magnified 100 times, stencils were made of it, then all two kilometres of those templates were printed out on tracing paper. Using the templates as a guideline, the designs were chalk-dusted onto the plane. About fourteen people painted that first Dreaming plane over a two-week period in Hangar 245 at Sydney Airport. We flew over from Adelaide to make sure the colours and their application were right. Then, just before the first flight to Kansai Airport, the Wunala Dreaming plane was wheeled out.

The flight schedule was changed, so that the plane would arrive at Kansai half an hour before Ansett's first flight, rather than half an hour after. The Wunala Dreaming plane landed at dusk on a very still evening, on 3 September 1994. There was just a slight haze. The first three people to come off were my relations – Yanyuwa dancers, my people. Roy Hammer came first, then Tom Simon, and then Barry John with the didgeridoo. They performed their traditional dance, to give the blessing of the Yanyuwa people. Musso was to have come too, but was taken ill. Although he wasn't able to join us, he said, 'You go on ahead. I'll wait here, you go on ahead.'

The impact of that plane was enormous. It's been of huge

benefit to Qantas, and to Australia – and, of course, we've had a great spin-off from it as well. Qantas still uses it for major promotions, things like inaugural flights to new destinations and announcing periodic results to the financial press. It's been fantastic for us and fantastic for Qantas.

After the first flight, the demand for the plane to fly the Japan routes grew, but they couldn't fly Wunala Dreaming to Japan regularly because it was a 747-400, which couldn't be serviced there. So Qantas commissioned us to paint a second plane. I was reluctant at first, because I didn't want a copycat plane. I needn't have worried – we did it completely differently, using a different palette of colours. The Nalanji Dreaming plane was launched twelve months later and it now flies regularly to Japan and all across Asia.

Today, other airlines are painting fuselages with all kinds of designs, but they don't seem to have the same impact as the trailblazing Qantas ones. In fact, those planes are the largest moving artworks anywhere in the world. Qantas has led the world on that. It took a little company like ours to convince them it was a good way to go.

Whenever I see those planes, they make me feel so Australian, and the standing they have in the world makes me feel good. Australians constantly tell us they feel good when they see those designs; it makes them feel at home when they see the planes in Los Angeles or Frankfurt or London. That's how we really like people to feel – good about Aboriginal art, about Australia.

Soaring

When I first saw the Wunala Dreaming plane I sort of melted inwardly. It's a feeling you don't get very often – it makes you feel humble, elated, secure. It makes you feel all those things. It's happiness, I suppose. Of course, having such an icon within an Australian company of such standing is a satisfying feeling. I get quite emotional when I see it. I don't think it's a feeling of triumph, really. I think of those hard times of my life still, but the Qantas planes belong to the good times; they are a powerful symbol of my struggle to promote my culture.

As far as acceptance of Aboriginal culture goes, the planes have sort of jumped a couple of generations. You couldn't imagine them being done in the 1960s. In the 1970s I think they should've been done, could've been done, but I suppose those sorts of things don't get done unless people are ready for it, or some people are ready for it.

It must have taken a great deal of courage on James Strong's part to push it and have his board accept it – and for the company, the rank and file, to be happy with it. It took a great deal of corporate strength and, of course, the support of Gary Pemberton, the chairman of the Qantas board. I think they've been rewarded because Qantas has grown from strength to strength, and I like to think Wunala Dreaming has played a part in that success.

Wunala is the generic word for kangaroo in the Yanyuwa language. What is depicted on the plane is the movement of the Kangaroo Spirit People across the landscape in its formative days, in the Dreamtime. It shows the pattern of movement over the country – dotting here, creating landforms there, bestowing the rich colours of the Australian landscape, from the orange sunsets to the green grass and the red earth. We've made it so it covers our region around Borroloola and extends across the land, right through to the red country.

Our Dreaming goes a long way with the kangaroo – and of course kangaroos are of strong significance not only to our mob but throughout the country. Where he travels you can see his tracks: he must have a feed, he must travel through the countryside, the vegetation. The plane depicts the landscape in our way; it's quite abstract and yet the symbol of the kangaroo is quite prominent.

The response from Aboriginal people has been very positive. Musso said, 'You've done good for our people and the Yanyuwa, Mara mob. Very good. Good for our people and for our tribe.' Sadly, my mother's blindness (her eyesight had been deteriorating since the late 1970s, as a result of glaucoma) meant she never saw the planes but she had them described to her by people who had. My mum was a very softly spoken lady and she didn't say much one way or another. She didn't comment directly to me, it wasn't her way, but I have no doubt a lot of my relatives' comments were coloured by my mother's opinion.

In fact, generally, there was very little criticism. I recall one comment by David McNicol in *The Bulletin* – but then I've always felt that he has a negative attitude towards things

Aboriginal. And Sir Bruce Watson, a National Australia Bank board member, spoke negatively to me about the plane at a function. Not that this surprised me, either – I don't think the National Australia Bank is very community-minded, or very Australian-minded.

My feeling is that we can't do many planes like that. It has to be really well thought out. I'm confident another one or two could be done so long as they were of distinct designs. We'd have to make them different and fresh again.

Through the two planes, we did some promotional work with Qantas. It was on one of those trips that I gained a deeper appreciation of how well Musso knew the land. He was with us on a Nalanji flight, on Qantas's 75th birthday. We all boarded the plane in Sydney for a public relations run, flew over Longreach, then flew over Surfers Paradise and back down to Sydney. And Musso, looking down at the landscape from the air, told me stories about that land, where he'd been a drover for many years. 'See that place there, Cunnamulla, I camped over there,' he said, pointing to a spot west of Cunnamulla.

He could pick it out all these years later. And he could pinpoint the spot where an Aboriginal man had been buried in a tree just near there. There we were, flying in this technological marvel of a Boeing 747-300 jet over the same land he traversed on a stock horse many years ago, and he's able to point out landmarks.

On a visit to Japan, Musso had, as usual, the presence of a statesman. People respected him for what he was and who he

was. That sort of treatment was not afforded to Musso throughout most of his life in Australia as a tribal Aboriginal man. I
suppose the important thing to Musso was that he was a big
man in his own sense; he didn't have to prove to anyone else
who he was.

In January 1995 we went to Borroloola for my mother's funeral.
Ros, Tim, James and Julia came with me. Many of the local
people were there. It was sad, very sad. I've been back to
Borroloola several times since, but Borroloola is not the same
without my mother. It's not the same without people like Musso
(who has also died), Old Tim, Jack Isaac and the other fellows
of their generation.

These days I'm a full member of the tribe but not living there,
so I can only assume a certain amount of authority. However,
that gives me a full participatory role in tribal business up there.
My opinion is sought for lots of things, particularly when they
cross over into the white system. On day-to-day matters,
though, 3000 kilometres is a long way away – and there's a great
potential for friction in that distance.

I know, too, that I still have a lot to learn. There is a lot out
there. I know that the practice of a lot of traditional things is
still kept underground. I know there are people who uphold the
law under instructions from the elders. They can bring about
justice and mete out punishment in the right place at the right

time. Sometimes this is killing outright by spear, other times death can be caused by methods that people might find hard to believe. People can be harmed by singing, some part of their body can become terribly heavy, something like that. Even a fingernail, hair or faeces can be used against you. You don't leave those things lying around.

Often, if you do something wrong, but face your punishment of a ritual spearing in the leg or whatever might be appropriate, everything's alright after that. You've paid your price and justice has been done.

Justice and punishment is only one aspect of the power of traditional Aboriginal practices, though. During my days with the Commonwealth Government in Canberra, I went to Yuendumu, north west of Alice Springs, and met quite a few Warlpiri people. One young man there, who was a Jagamara, asked me, 'Where do you come from?'

I told him, 'Borroloola.'

He was okay with that. We got on very well. Then I went back a second time and he remembered me. He said, 'Hey, can you teach me some of those songs from Borroloola?'

He'd heard about the strength of the songs from Borroloola, and he wanted to sing this woman he'd fallen in love with; he wanted to make her fall in love with him. He wanted to sing these very powerful love songs he wanted me to teach him, but I couldn't; it wouldn't have been right. I don't know if he ever got that woman, either.

I do know one of those songs. I'm not saying I've ever used it, but I do know that it works. I've known other tribes in the centre of Australia to have it too.

I don't have as strong a grasp of the ceremonies as the people who live there all the time, but I can participate in the dances. I'm considered an elder now, a malbu, and I don't necessarily have to do the dancing, so I'm privileged in that way. It's appropriate that I know the dances, particularly as they relate to me and my immediate group, and I know the things I should be a part of. I can't really divulge any more than that. Suffice to say that my knowledge is significant to the tribe and it's very important to me.

What really worries me is that a lot of the culture is dying out. I suppose I'm contributing to that by not living there all the time, and by not having a good enough command of the language to grasp all the nuances. Having been taken away contributes as well. I feel I should play a greater role and I feel inadequate in some areas where I should be filling in the gaps.

A lot of the younger people should be contributing more to gaining that knowledge and maintaining the system for future generations as well. They're not doing as much as they should. It's easy for me to criticise, but I do realise there are a lot of pressures on them. The young men don't feel as if they are a strong part of either system and this affects their self-esteem. As a consequence, they're not picking up and continuing the songs, ceremonies and the culture with enough depth. Our people and people in neighbouring areas used to perform the ceremonies with strength and vigour and they knew the exact protocol to make sure ceremonies took place across all the neighbouring tribal areas too.

Instead, these days, there is a drift away: the younger people who go out for schooling, for instance, often move out. They're marrying people from outside the area as well – from Tennant Creek, Darwin and further afield again. The movement is quite extensive.

Sickness has also taken its toll, as has the change in diet. People go to the local chicken shop for takeaway food, soft drinks and hamburgers. It's not just an occasional treat, it's daily and it's supplanting the traditional diet, which was pretty well balanced and which led to the long and healthy lives of people like Old Tim and Old Donegan, those people that were alive when I was a kid and way beyond. They lived to their nineties and upwards. Nowadays, in our region, the low fifties is the average lifespan of an Aboriginal man. We've got a number of people on kidney machines and obesity is a problem. These chronic conditions have decimated a couple of generations, so we now have a disproportionate number of younger people and a few older people and not a great deal in between, none of those middle-aged or upper-middle-aged people.

All of these things are contributing to our culture not being passed on. The dominant culture has an impact, too, in the way it restricts the ability of Aboriginal people to move across the land. School, gaols, police systems and changing land owner-ship, even TV, mean they can't or don't practise ceremonies in the old traditional land areas. Fortunately, in Borroloola we have a few parcels of land that we can claim as our own, that we have title over. Our group was more fortunate with land than a lot of others in this country and that's enabled us to maintain ceremonies and movement in some areas. That's the case with most communities in the Top End. Even today, white settlement is quite limited and hasn't completely extinguished Aboriginal culture.

I can't imagine my children will move back there, though. Tim's very keen on computer animation and composing music for films. That's his interest at this point in time. James wants to do commerce. Julia is only eleven, but already she wants to be an athlete. What can they do in a place like Borroloola? The Internet may help but I'm not sure if face-to-face contact will be replaced by computers in the very near future.

Where our company has been having most success is in taking Aboriginal culture to the world – especially when we've considered an idea and promoted it ourselves. We still have to come up with the concept, then think how it can best be used in a corporate context, but that's the way we tend to do things. At the Atlanta Olympics, for example, we put Balarinji designs on a two-metre-high Coca-Cola bottle for an exhibition in the Coca-Cola museum. That was not a huge money spinner, it was more the promotion of our brand name – getting the design out there was our primary aim. We made contact with Coca-Cola and developed a dialogue until it eventually came into fruition.

We had no problem using Aboriginal design in this way, not

in a philosophical sense. If you can't market your products, you'll never succeed. In my view marketing is something Aboriginal people must come to terms with. If we base it on quality and integrity, there's no problem.

Relocating our business to Sydney in 1997 was a good move, too. Compared to Adelaide, living in a city like Sydney is a lot more pressured, but it has done a great deal to raise the company's profile and enable it to expand. Every month we're finding great opportunities. Recently, we've done the Christmas and Millennium branding for the City of Sydney, the inaugural work of art for Stadium Australia, and the design and signage for the Bank of America's Olympic Tour throughout the USA, emphasising the indigenous culture of Australia, the host nation of the 2000 Olympics. Added to that, I'm currently chair of the National Aboriginal Sports Corporation of Australia and vice-chairman of the Commercial Development Corporation, which provides venture capital to Aboriginal groups. If anything, the pace of life is getting faster.

These days I feel secure in both Aboriginal and non-Aboriginal camps. There is an element of reconciliation between the two – in my own feelings and in how I relate both to being Aboriginal and to the white system. One of the things, though, is I'm still not sure how much I've suffered as a result of my early upbringing, when we were constantly being told that the Aboriginal culture was no good.

I've always identified as an Aborigine but I've always had to keep some things hidden inside myself; I've been forced to conceal my sense of Aboriginality. I haven't been able to communicate in my own language from the time I was four, except for the times that I go back to Borroloola. I really don't know how much I've buried so deeply that not even I can find it. I do know that I've put a lot of things out of my mind from those very harsh times. I remember lots of things, but some of the bad things I've blocked out. Have I countered that trauma psychologically by seeking solace in traditional Aboriginal culture? Who knows?

Overwhelmingly, I feel I got back into my culture because I wanted to. A lot of my contemporaries did not identify with their Aboriginality like I did, and I feel they've had a very trying time with their own lives. Some have become alcoholics and some have died premature deaths. Maybe it is a little simplistic, but part of me wonders whether they got into difficulties because they couldn't find the inner serenity that would enable them to take pride in their Aboriginal heritage.

My pride in my culture sustains me, but who knows how much more I could have had if I'd been raised by my own people. Even as I was playing soccer at a young age – at a time when being an Aborigine was considered a stigma – when I was referred to in the press as Aboriginal, I was very comfortable with that. It's what enabled me to play that little bit extra – I felt proud all the time. I keep telling my kids, 'Always be proud of your heritage – whether it's the part of you that's Aboriginal, or Irish, or Tasmanian.' It's going to be hard for them if they try not to be Aboriginal because of their colour. Tim could perhaps get away with it a little more than the other two, but Tim is very secure in the fact that he is Aboriginal, as are the other two.

There have been times with our business when it was commercially expedient for me not to be at the forefront of going to clients to sell products and ideas. Yet I've never denied that I was an Aborigine and I think that's always been a strength.

I admit I'll walk away from a possible confrontation when someone says, 'Oh, you're a nigger, you black so-and-so.' I won't react in a way they would expect. The reason is I've always strived for the war to be won, rather than the individual battles. It's a strategy I've adopted, a mind-set where I'll react in certain ways in particular situations.

When some kid was antagonistic in the schoolroom, I used to have fights. I won more than I lost, but what was I going to do – fight physical fights all my life? I learned when I was pretty young that if you hit, you get hit back: eye for an eye, tooth for a tooth, that sort of thing. I didn't see any future in that. Sure I can win a few fights but the rules that you are playing by are their rules. My overriding rule was 'I must survive'.

The world is bigger than any individual I have a problem with at any moment in time.

On the soccer field, when I was abused for being black, the simple solution might have been to go and physically have it out with them, but my solution was to show exactly what I was made of – I'd humiliate them with sheer skill or speed. I'd beat them in the game that mattered to them.

It's been a long war and for me it is still going. I feel I'm on top of a lot of things but the Aboriginal issues are still bubbling underneath – I don't think their complex nature has been understood, even by a lot of Aborigines. A lot of our people have lost the war and a lot of the whites who indulge in racism have lost it, too.

Meanwhile, the situation has changed because the community has become more global. Whereas years ago we were fighting mainly on a one-dimensional level and had common enemies, now some of those enemies have changed and become our allies. It's these things that mean we always have to reassess our direction for the future.

I know my kids won't have to fight the same battles I've had. They keep telling me that. 'We're not living back in your days, Dad. You know it's a different ball game. You've lost the plot in a lot of those areas.' I suppose they're right in some ways, but old traditions die hard. I can only go by my own experiences. I'm sure my kids will come around to aspects of my way of thinking but I'm also going to go a fair way towards their way of thinking. That's a healthy thing. You must keep learning.

Since meeting my cousin John Moriarty in Tralee, I've found out that he had two brothers living in London – Dennis and Michael. I've met up with them as well and they've given me a lot of information about my Irish family. We still keep in touch.

In January 1999 Ros, the kids and I were in London, staying in Highgate, and we invited my relatives for dinner. Jane

Monaghan, Dennis's daughter, who's a talented interior decorator, was there with her husband and her son, as well as Michael and his boys.

We put on a big meal and there were twelve Moriartys there, including three John Moriartys. It was great sitting around that table listening to my cousins. They sang songs, told jokes, they were full of life. We had grilled salmon and Ros cooked baked fruit – pears soaked in red wine. The meal was delicious and, for me, the family gathering was just as fulfilling.

These days we keep getting invitations – to dinners, weddings. I think family is such an important aspect of life that you must make the effort to maintain it. It's important for your kids, for their stability, for them to know exactly who they are, where they come from and what obligations they have in the family sense. They should have that knowledge without it stifling their own lives.

Family is important and I feel good with it. I like to be sure of my complete identity. After what the system did to me, it's doubly important.

I've only gone to sleep once before my kids, and that was only a few weeks ago. I found it strange to go to bed before them but I was so tired I just had to go to sleep. I may be overly protective and worry unduly, but that's part of the legacy I have to live with. I still have broken sleep. Sometimes there's a nightmare or two and I get up and go around and check on everybody. I suppose that's normal with families, isn't it? The kids have a go at me in a gentle way – they're always telling me that I worry too much, but I don't think they mind me worrying about them really. Ros is accepting; she's very good like that.

I don't think I've ever told my Irish relatives about what happened to me, about the circumstances of my being taken away. I might have in passing to John but not to Michael or Dennis. I think it's because when I've been with them, renewing family ties, I've wanted to dwell on positive things.

I still celebrate my birthday on April Fools' Day, though. My family want me to have it on another day but I don't want to change it. I don't apologise for that – and no-one has apologised to me for it either. After all I've come through, in its own small way it serves as a reminder of what was done to me.

On Australia Day 2000 I was fortunate to receive an Order of Australia (AM). I am honoured by the award and equally proud to accept it as an Aboriginal and as an Australian. While I don't expect or seek such recognition, it was gratifying for me, my family and my people. I was especially happy to receive it for the things that are important to me – political advocacy, promotion of indigenous art and culture, and contribution to business.

I was also pleased and excited to be selected as one of the torch bearers for the 2000 Olympic Games in Sydney. Sport has been good to me and I look forward to celebrating the Australian games.

Yet, while I have found my peace in both camps – the indigenous community and the wider Australia community – 2000 and 2001 are crossroads years for all of us. For this nation of Australia to come of age, there must be a reconciliation of past treatment of indigenous people. I believe that the majority of Australians have a sincere desire to resolve the disadvantage faced by the indigenous minority. But for reconciliation to move forward, Aborigines and Torres Strait Islanders also need to come to the negotiating table in a genuine spirit of cooperation. There is a lot of money going into indigenous affairs today, and it is my view that a small number of Aborigines in key positions would not be proponents of positive change if it undermined their income, power base and authority. I am conscious of many aspects of black–white relations and indigenous politics that will need to change if we are to come together in mutual respect. Solidarity based only on poverty and oppression can be a bitter and destructive force.

Things have moved on since the 1960s when we made our pilgrimages to Canberra in the name of change. The fight for equality and acceptance is not yet won, but we have come a long way. It is heartening that the Council for Aboriginal Reconciliation has attracted widespread support for its agenda of unity. Our Balarinji artwork for the Council depicts two outstretched hands – one from the sea and one from the land, both reaching towards the centre of the painting. I wanted it to serve as a reminder that as a community we can only bridge the divide by meeting each other half way. It also symbolises my personal journey with Balarinji – to create designs that celebrate a young nation's connection to its ancient past.

I stay close to my tribe and family in Borroloola. Willy O'Keefe, my late stepfather, had extensive ceremonial links with Jingili tribal country. He belonged to the Dungkumini, a dangerous Lightning Dreaming ceremony that was practised on a property called Balbirini, 100 kilometres south-west of Borroloola. In 1999 I learned that, before his death in 1997, Willy had ensured that my children and I were included in statutory documentation as traditional owners of Balbirini. When he was still alive, Willy often told me that he wanted my family to maintain links with his traditional land. The children are excited about belonging to Balbirini, and take it seriously. I am happy for them that they will be able to keep their connection with Borroloola. Most importantly, this ceremonial link will tie them and their children, and perhaps even their children's children, to the spiritual essence of the culture of my people. My culture.

I feel as if my life has turned full circle.

Index

Index

Index

Index

Index

Index

Index